CORPS
BUSINE

Other Books by David H. Freedman

*Brainmakers: How Scientists Are Moving Beyond Computers
to Create a Rival to the Human Brain*

At Large: The Strange Case of the World's Biggest Internet Invasion
(with Charles C. Mann)

CORPS
BUSINESS

THE 30 MANAGEMENT
PRINCIPLES OF THE
U.S. MARINES

DAVID H. FREEDMAN

HarperBusiness
An Imprint of HarperCollins*Publishers*

A hardcover edition of this book was published in 2000 by HarperBusiness, an imprint of HarperCollins Publishers.

First paperback edition published 2001.

Designed by William Ruoto

Library of Congress Cataloging-in-Publication Data
Freedman, David H., 1954–
 Corps Business: the 30 management principles of the U.S. Marines / David H. Freedman—1st ed.
  p. cm.
 Originally published: New York: HarperBusiness, c2000.
 Includes bibliographical references and index.
 ISBN 0-06-661979-3
 1. United States Marine Corps—Management. 2. Management. I. Title
VE23.F74 20001
658.4—dc21   00-054135

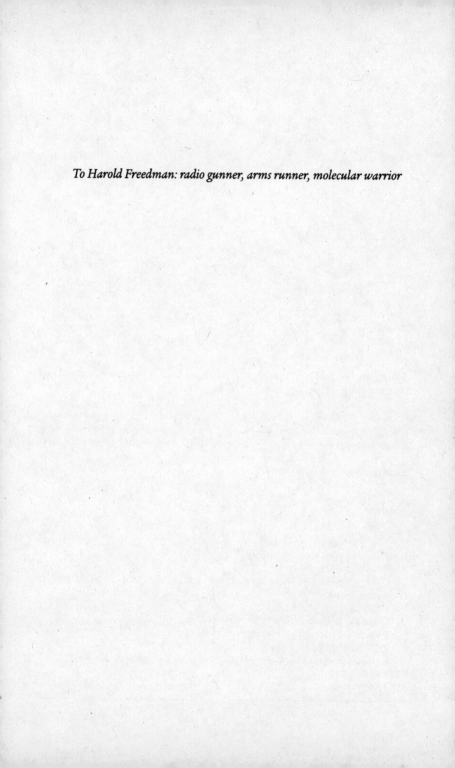

To Harold Freedman: radio gunner, arms runner, molecular warrior

CONTENTS

THE LEADERSHIP IMPERATIVE

By General Charles C. Krulak,
Thirty-first Commandant, U.S. Marine Corps

For two hundred and twenty-three years, the Marine Corps has performed two crucial and inextricably linked tasks for our nation: it makes Marines and wins battles. Indeed, the title "Marine" has become synonymous with victory. Today's Marine joins the select company of many generations of proud warriors. In once-obscure places like Belleau Wood, Iwo Jima, and Chosin Reservoir, Marines have proven their mettle time and again.

Marines have long recognized the unequivocal link between battlefield success and leadership. The Corps has therefore placed a premium on those qualities of character integral to effective and positive leadership and has strived to nurture them in all Marines. There is no higher compliment than to be called a leader of Marines. It is combat leadership that defines the Corps' ethos—its cherished core values of honor, courage, and commitment.

Despite its enviable legacy, the Corps has not rested. It cannot afford to. The challenges facing our country are too compelling to permit complacency, and the Corps has remained committed to its relentless pursuit of excellence in leadership.

The nation's security challenges are changing at the blinding speed that characterizes the Information Age. The rapid diffusion of technology, rampant transnational threats, and the consequences of globalization have changed the strategic landscape and levied tremendous demands on the military. Urban areas, burdened by 70 percent of the world's population and some of them incapable of providing essential infrastructure and support, are becoming the world's flashpoints and the likely war zones of the future. In such an environment, chaos will often rule and our adversaries will multiply yet become less conspicuous.

Confounded by our conventional superiority, these often faceless enemies will resort to asymmetric methods to identify and exploit our vulnerabilities. The tragic bombings of the U.S. embassies in Nairobi and Dares Salaam dramatically illustrated the pervasiveness of such threats. Though it is impossible to gauge precisely the character of tomorrow's security landscape, the evidence strongly suggests that it will grow increasingly hostile and perplexing. In the twenty-first century, America will rely more heavily than ever before on an agile force in readiness: a Corps of keenly trained, equipped, and organized Marines prepared to respond to an infinite array of contingencies spanning the entire spectrum of conflict.

In the past decade the strategic, operational, and tactical levels of war have begun to merge perceptibly. Consequently the actions of the individual Marine, the true "tip of the spear," have assumed greater significance and can now have profound strategic implications. Contemporary crisis responses, such as Operation Restore Hope in Somalia, are exceedingly complex and often combine the disparate challenges of operations other than war with those of mid-intensity conflict. Modern crises therefore are infinitely challenging and amorphous and represent what the Corps has metaphorically described as the "three-block war"—Marines may confront the entire gamut of tactical challenges within the narrow confines of three contiguous city blocks.

Operating "far from the flagpole," without the direct supervision of senior leadership but under the unforgiving scrutiny of the media, our young Marines must be ingrained with the qualities of character necessary to permit effective, independent decisionmaking under extreme stress. As often as not, the truly difficult situations confronting them will not relate to traditional military concerns but will be moral quandaries whose resolution requires a high degree of maturity, discretion, and judgment. The outcome of any future operation, whether humanitarian assistance, peacekeeping, or traditional warfighting, will often rest at the lowest level—with the rifleman or fire team—and with their ability to make the right moral decision. On the complex, asymmetrical battlefields of the twenty-first century, effective decentralized control and execution will be essential to mission success. Acknowledging this reality, the Corps has reinvigorated its efforts to develop in Marines the leadership skills needed to deal with the high-stakes challenges of the three-block war.

The process of building a Marine leader begins with building a Marine. Marines are forged, one hammer blow at a time, in a combat-proven process conceived to instill within the heart of each a burning appreciation for our core values. The rigor of recruit and officer candidate training is capable of transforming an American youth and preparing him or her for the challenges of service to country.

The hallmark of this fertile environment for personal and professional development is pervasive, clearly defined, and universally respected standards of conduct. These standards stress personal accountability, and our faithful adherence to them has distinguished the Corps for more than two centuries. Their influence is inescapable and shapes our every action. The product of this priceless admixture of quality people, rigorous training, and fairly enforced, traditional standards is exceptionally capable Marines of resolute character. The process plants within them the seed for lifelong growth. The Corps does not claim to create character within its members, but it builds on an existing foundation within a challenging atmosphere conducive to the fullest expression of the individual's native ability.

Leadership cannot be learned in the same manner in which competency is developed with a piece of equipment. There are no checklists, matrices, or shortcuts to effective leadership. It is truly a lifelong work in progress. The Corps has recognized that the qualities of individual character revealed in the crucible of entry-level training must be polished, strengthened, and sustained. A challenging yet supportive environment, conducive to the expression of initiative, tolerant of mistakes, and unsullied by any vestige of a "zero-defects" mentality, is essential for that purpose. Our method is surprisingly simple: Marines are thrust into such an arena and compelled to lead. They are given meaningful responsibility and a modicum of supervision, and they are held strictly accountable for their actions. The results of this most basic of approaches speak for themselves.

It is worth noting that in the Corps leadership is not the purview of an elite—it is the business of everyone. All Marines possess manifold obligations, extending both up and down the chain of command, to seniors and juniors alike. Every Marine is at heart a teacher and mentor, obliged to pass on his knowledge and the benefit of his experience to his subordinates. General John A. Lejeune, the thirteenth commandant of the Marine Corps, long ago captured the essence of the special bond between senior and junior when he likened it to "the nature of the relation between father and son." Leaders at every level are expected to be deeply involved in the development of their subordinates and must firmly guide the growth of leadership within them.

Leadership, even within the military, is a social contract in the purest sense of the expression, predicated equally on the leader's desire to lead and on the consent of those led. It is grounded in the subordinate's trust in the leader and the institution. The leader, therefore, must clearly demonstrate the true underpinning of his moral authority—his unquestionable character. The subordinate's faith in the leader's integrity must not be violated.

We must also consider why Marines lead. The answer is straightforward: they lead because they are obliged to do so. The unmistakable lesson of the past is that leadership is integral to success on the battlefield. As such, it is the most rewarding of privileges afforded them; leadership is simply a Marine's raison d'être. Marines are ultimately judged by the quality of their leadership and by the quality of the leadership reflected in their subordinates. A complex phenomenon, nearly defying description, leadership is fundamentally a reflection of an individual's values, education, training, and experience. It is the precious amalgam of his or her lifelong efforts at personal and professional improvement. It is above all else a product of character.

David Freedman has described Marine Corps training as "the best management training program in America." I believe, as does he, that our methods have applicability in the business world. Certainly there is a fundamental difference between military leadership and business management: the Corps endeavors to build leaders who are prepared to deal with life-and-death challenges. The Corps is also, however, building versatile leaders capable of handling all challenges, including that of managing in the traditional sense. Conversely the Corps has recognized the utility of certain business practices and has frequently turned to industry, commerce, and academia for insights. Clearly there is common ground between Marine leadership and business management.

In the following pages, Mr. Freedman accurately captures the essence of Marine Corps leadership and thoroughly describes our unique approach to leadership training. I am convinced that leadership is the common currency of the military, industry, government, and academia, and that versatile leaders of character are the linchpin of all successful enterprises.

Semper Fidelis,

General Charles C. Krulak
Thirty-first Commandant, U.S. Marine Corps

ACKNOWLEDGMENTS

Mark Campagna, an officer in the U.S. Naval Reserve and a brother-in-law first class, suggested to me during a run that I take a look at the Marines if I wanted to know something about excellence and innovation in management. If he hadn't, this book wouldn't exist.

George Gendron, Jeff Seglin, and others at *Inc.* magazine helped turn a vague idea into the article that served as a springboard to this book.

Rick Balkin once again overstepped his bounds, serving not merely as a wise and supportive agent but also as a good friend and deft editor.

There are still publishing house editors who are dedicated to providing just the right combination of encouragement, freedom, and constructive criticism. One of them is named Dave Conti. I suspect part of his secret is having Devi Pillai for an assistant.

Journalist/friends Charles Mann and Sarah Schafer offered support at crucial moments throughout the project.

David Abrahamson, a long-time close friend and something of an expert on the military, provided invaluable advice and perspective.

Rachel, Alex, and Jason were enthusiastic and contagious appreciators of Marine-related information and memorabilia. It wouldn't have been nearly as much fun otherwise.

It would take a book in itself to detail all the ways in which my wife, Laurie Tobey-Freedman, contributed.

I am foremost indebted to the Marines for their time, energy, and candor. I regret to say there are simply too many individual Marines (including former Marines) who cooperated with me to thank them all by name here. Many are mentioned in the text, but in an effort to avoid bombarding the reader with a stream of unfamiliar names, I have committed the crime of leaving many more anonymous. Here are just a handful of the otherwise unnamed, in recognition of the fact that these people are among those who took on more than their share of the burden that I represented, and did so without even so much as hinting that they might have other things to do: Capt. Sean Clements, Capt. Sean Gibson, Lt. Col. Jenny Holbert, Lt. Rob James, Lt. Col. Betsy Judge, Lt. Billy Mitchell, gunny Stephen Mullinax, Capt. Mike Neumann, Capt. Sam Nunnick, Capt. Doug Powell, Lt. Patty Restrepo. There are many, many others.

Though I hold up the Marine Corps' capabilities and practices in this book, it is in no way my intention to do so at the expense of the other branches of the United States military. Marines themselves are usually quick to point out that when it comes to more sustained, larger-scale, more conventional conflicts, the Army, Navy, and Air Force are well suited to the task. If anything in this book appears to imply a lack of the highest regard for the other branches and the people who serve proudly in them, then I apologize for expressing myself poorly.

Finally, I'd like to point out that I recognize that Marines haven't given their lives so that businesses can become more competitive. I hope that in trying to provide a frame of reference linking Marine Corps' practices with the needs of corporations I haven't given the impression that I've lost sight of the fact that the Marines operate for far higher stakes and for a deeper purpose. It's for this reason, more than any other, that I am indebted to them.

INTRODUCTION

This is not a gentlemanly century;
this is a century whose primary business is war.
—ALBERT EINSTEIN

For many managers, business has become a nightmare of velocity and complexity. In the technology sector, companies leap into existence and steal significant market share from established companies in a matter of weeks. Twitches in a hyperactive stock market whisk high-flying financial services firms to the edge of bankruptcy. Movie studios rise or fall on their ability to manufacture a few days' worth of good buzz. Pharmaceutical companies lose a million dollars each day a new drug is late to market and risk being beaten to the punch altogether by any of hundreds of tiny biotech firms. Automakers are under pressure to slash two or more years off the development cycle for new car models and to have the capacity to assemble cars from parts ordered a few days before. Broadcast networks are forced to scramble for alliances as their audiences are whittled away by a mushrooming array of cable networks and online services. And in every industry, better informed and more demanding customers are proving their willingness to switch their business at the blink of a Web banner to any company that can muster up a slight edge in price, service, selection, or quality.

The result: companies are desperate to be nimbler. Organizations that can't react quickly and effectively to the threats and opportunities popping up all around them are finding themselves out of the game.

One might suppose that the military, with its legendarily hierar-chical command-and-control habits, would be the last place to look for nimbleness. No wonder: the Army, Navy, and Air Force have evolved over the past nine decades to fight world wars, in the expecta-tion of having many months to plan and deploy and perhaps years to settle conflicts. When the media reported in April 1999 during the Kosovo bombing that the Army needed at least a month to ready a dozen or so Apache helicopters for action in the campaign, managers all over America must have been thinking that this sort of reaction time would never cut it in the business world.

These same managers might assume that the Marine Corps is the most hidebound military branch of all. Certainly the Marines have earned the public's deep respect as the nation's toughest combat force. Even younger people unaware of the Marines' astounding record of World War II victories in the hellish beach invasions of the Pacific islands generally recognize Marines as proud, well-trained, ferocious fighters. But Marines are also widely imagined to be rigid, almost mindlessly aggressive soldiers ready to hurl themselves straight at the enemy under the orders of abusive, blood-and-guts officers.

In fact, in spite of the boot camp images of snarling drill instruc-tors and compliant, shaved-head recruits that are so deeply ingrained in the popular culture, the Marine Corps is one of the most open-minded, innovative, knowledge-oriented, and in some ways free-wheeling organizations in the world. The Corps' ability to react quickly and effectively in environments seething with complex, unpredictable, and fast-changing threats and opportunities would make the average Silicon Valley start-up seem hidebound. It's the Marines' specialty. If they weren't good at it, they would, at best, have been subsumed into the Army or, at worst, become casualties in large numbers.

The Marines are given America's most challenging combat mis-sions, including beach invasions and urban combat. In addition, the Corps has taken responsibility for tricky, often poorly defined nonwar missions ranging from evacuating embassies to providing humanitarian aid under hostile conditions. In short, the Marines have specialized in operating under chaotic, fast-changing, high-intensity conditions that provide not only little way of knowing what the opposition is going to throw at you but perhaps no way of knowing exactly who the opposition is going to be. Reaction plans have to be drawn up and implemented on the spot, under fire, and with little margin for error.

All this will have a familiar ring to many managers. As an example of what businesses are up against, consider that a few years ago, according to the *New York Times*, companies in the computer industry had begun to operate under "Netscape time"—a reference to the way Netscape's nimble business style had shrunk product life cycles in response to rapid fluctuations in the Internet software market. Months later Netscape itself was surprised by competitive maneuvers from Microsoft, couldn't respond quickly enough, and was soon in a tailspin from which it never recovered. Apparently Netscape time was too slow.

Everything about the Marines—their culture, their organizational structure, their management style, their logistics, their decisionmaking process—is geared toward high-speed, high-complexity environments. It's Darwinian: with no less than their survival as an institution and as individual human beings at stake, the Marines have had to examine, discard, redefine, refine, and rerefine their approaches to achieve the ultimate in rapid, effective response to dynamic challenges.

Can some of these approaches be transported to the business world? When we think of companies that have been run under by former military officers, the example that often springs to mind is EDS, founded by Ross Perot (who served in the Navy) and famous for its rigid, conservative style. But there's little that is Marine-like about EDS. Instead, think of Chrysler, which went from the edge of bankruptcy in 1989 to become the world's most profitable carmaker, a transformation largely credited to a push by its president, Robert Lutz—a former Marine—to develop a hot new line of innovative cars in unheard-of turnaround times. Another example is Federal Express, a virtual icon of business speed and effectiveness, founded and run by the former Marine Fred Smith. (Seen on a T-shirt at a Marine base: "The U.S. Marines: When it absolutely, positively has to be destroyed overnight.")

Smith and Lutz brought many of the Marine management principles with them when they jumped to the business world. This book will familiarize managers who don't happen to be former Marines with the same principles.

I should point out that the set of principles that I identify are not explicitly taught by the Marines in their schools or quoted by them in training or publications. (Indeed, Marines rarely use the term "management.") The principles represent my own take on what underlies Marine practices, based on more than one hundred interviews with Marines of all ranks and many days spent observing them in training and exercises. In other words, these principles are not necessarily what the Marines *say* they do but what they *actually* do—and have been doing in some cases for decades and even centuries.

The Marine Corps management principles are built around simple truths about human nature and the uncertainties of dynamic environments. Obviously these are factors that can have a great impact on any organization. The difference is that the Marines have staked their lives on them. That's pretty good motivation for getting it right.

☆ ☆ ☆ ☆ ☆

1. PLANNING AND DECISION-MAKING

Hope is not a course of action.
—USMC COLONEL MICHAEL O'NEAL

The airstream rips through the open bays of the CH-53 Superstallion, extorting a layer of tears through which to regard the crumpled-tin-foil ocean, burnished by cloud shadows, streaking by below. Conversation is impossible over the thunderous drone of the convenience-store-sized helicopter, and it's beside the point anyway. Seated shoulder to shoulder in two facing rows are fifteen mostly young people in casually neat dress, as if on a trip to a museum, though that wouldn't explain the several duffel bags stuffed with assault rifles. The job in front of them is a delicate one: upon landing, they will have to thread their way to the U.S. embassy, without attracting the attention of unruly mobs or roving bands of thugs, and set up a communications center that will support the deployment of a few hundred of their colleagues.

At this moment many of those colleagues are just below decks from the helicopter's departure point on the USS *Tarawa*. Some are trying on the black ski masks they will wear when they storm a terrorist weapons cache. Others are checking the mortars they will use, if necessary, to defend a food supply intended for the starving locals. Still others are going over the maps that will help them locate and rescue the pilot of a downed jet.

The Marines are coming.

It's only an exercise—these Marines are invading a portion of the vast tracts of Camp Pendleton just north of San Diego. But no one is taking the missions lightly. For one thing, many of them have been up half the night making plans and preparations because the mission orders didn't even arrive until late the previous evening. For another, this exercise will provide the challenges of a real mission down to the smallest detail, including the thudding of real bullets into the ground around them. They don't know what awaits them onshore, but they are confident that six hours of planning and preparing have left them better equipped to face whatever it is than most military units would be with six months to get ready. If past experience is any guide, they are right.

Altogether, these Marines will carry out twenty-seven missions during the exercise; each assignment is not only plausible but in fact similar to an actual assignment taken on by the Corps in recent years. The missions run the gamut from large-scale combat, surgical strikes, and police actions to search-and-destroy operations, evacuations, and humanitarian assistance.

Anyone who wants to get a sense of the extent to which Marines have injected extraordinary levels of velocity, flexibility, and competence into their management practices could hardly do better than to observe a pre-mission planning session. We observe such a session in this chapter, gaining along the way an orientation to the basic Marine operating environment and mindset.

The unlit cigar bobs and jerks in Colonel Thomas Moore's mouth as he surveys the cramped and visibly rocking room. When he finally removes the cigar for a moment, the end is seen to have been ground to the flatness of cardboard. "The fight's on," he rumbles heartily. "How're y'all doin'?" The responses, and Moore's responses to the responses, vary from sounds that approximate a seal bark, a warthog growl, and a foghorn to, most frequently, the sound "oo-rah." Apparently the meeting is in order.

We are in the bowels of the *Tarawa*, the evening before the heli-copter journey. Many of the Marines' theories on decentralization and decisionmaking are about to be put to the test. The players are the members of the Eleventh MEU, or Marine Expeditionary Unit, under Moore's command. ("MEU" is pronounced, deceptively, the way a kitten would say it.) A MEU generally consists of about three ships' worth of Marines, jets, helicopters, artillery, tanks, amphibious and ground vehicles, weapons, and supplies. All Marines consider themselves part of a rapid deployment force. But a MEU is yet another level of rapid response. They are floating invasion parties.

Three 2,000-person MEUs are constantly springing in and out of existence from the pool of Marines at Camp Pendleton, another three out of Camp Lejeune, and three more out of Okinawa. Of the three MEUs associated with each location, one is deployed at sea, one is preparing to relieve it, and one is being taken apart. Of the three MEUs that are deployed, one is ordinarily stationed in the West Pacific, one in the Mediterranean, and one in the Persian Gulf.

Typically the MEUs just float around for most of their six-month deployments while the Marines on board do their best to keep them-selves occupied—they don't have many duties, since the ships are run by the Navy, and there isn't enough room for training exercises. So they read, lift weights, and occasionally, as a treat, get to practice their riflery skills on deck. It's a little like prison, except for the riflery part. But the Marines also know that if there's a summons for help, they could be landing on a beach under a hail of machine-gun fire in a matter of hours. Because they're typically the first ones to arrive at the scene of a military intervention, Marines in MEUs like to call themselves "the pointy tip of the spear" (though the term isn't exclu-sively reserved for MEUs).

Moore's MEU is finishing the end of its training cycle. But before it is allowed to deploy to the Persian Gulf or elsewhere, it has to get through two days of evaluation exercises, during which it will carry out the twenty-seven missions—a seemingly overwhelming number of assignments. At any one time as many as four missions will be under way simultaneously. The goal is to make the exercises more demanding than anything these Marines are likely to see in a real crisis. The Marines know roughly what sorts of tasks the exercises will address, but they are clueless as to the exact missions, the order in which the missions will hit, and the obstacles that will be thrown at them.

The performance of the MEU, and by implication of Moore and his staff, will be evaluated by their counterparts from a sister MEU that has recently returned from deployment. These other officers know better than anyone what a well-trained MEU should be able to accomplish; what's more, observing Moore's MEU, whether it succeeds or messes up, will provide a learning experience in its own right for these officers. (Moore and his staff will return the favor within a year.) The Marines call such exercises "evolutions," with all of the word's implication of inevitable, endless progress.

It is 8:00 P.M., and the first three mission orders have just been radioed to the *Tarawa*. One order calls for the Marines to set up a humanitarian aid operation in a poor country that has been devastated by floods, leading to starvation and disease. A second order calls for seizing a heavily guarded cache of weapons kept by terrorists, and a third directs them to recover a downed pilot. Each order is parceled out to a separate, quickly assembled "crisis action team" of about twelve people. Moore, who drops in on the teams by turn, is visiting the humanitarian assistance team. In less than an hour he will decide how that mission should be carried out.

FAST REACTION

All organizations face crises sooner or later. A competitor slashes prices in half; the firm's biggest customer jumps ship; a key supplier goes off-line. But do businesses need to react with the sort of lightning speed that the Marines aim for?

Consider Coca-Cola, a company so large, so well established, and so fortified by income from what may be the world's steadiest product that it might seem preposterous to suggest that it needs to worry about ultra-high-speed mission planning. Yet if Coca-Cola doesn't have fast-strike decision-making teams, it certainly wished it did in 1999 when word got out that a handful of consumers in Belgium had become violently ill from drinking allegedly contaminated Coke. Sales plummeted, and the company ultimately took a large hit to earnings—largely because it didn't react quickly and effectively in the first days, and even hours, of the scare.

Interestingly, Coca-Cola has proven itself capable of moving extremely quickly in the realm of marketing. When Princess Diana died in a car accident in 1997, the company immediately pulled together focus groups to get a fix on the public's emotions—a need to mourn balanced by a need to celebrate life, as it turned out—and then threw together a Coke ad campaign designed to be in sync with these feelings.

SPEEDING THE DECISION-MAKING PROCESS

Moore looks like Harrison Ford on steroids; his eyes bore in a way that's not unfriendly but seems to dare you to break eye contact, and even when he's grinning at you from fifteen feet away it still feels like he's in your face. Yet his presence appears to light up every Marine in sight. One lieutenant tells me that he had been thinking of leaving the Corps until he was assigned to Moore; now he says he doesn't mind the idea of "making the ultimate sacrifice." It takes a moment for it to sink in that this young man has just said he admires his boss enough to die for him. (Such sentiments are not entirely unheard of in the business world: in 1998, when a manager at Applied Management Systems in Rockville, Maryland, lost kidney function, a subordinate offered to donate one of hers.)

Moore's role is probably the most closely analogous in the Marines to that of a CEO. Marine generals are in some ways more like members of a company's board of directors, focusing on broader, long-term issues and leaving day-to-day management to the line executives. Moore's authority in the MEU is absolute. "I own everyone in this MEU," he says matter-of-factly. "And they own me." But Moore seems more comfortable with his charges than most CEOs do with their employees. An observer unaware of Moore's rank might easily mistake him for an early-middle-aged, unusually forceful and charismatic enlisted man as he strides through the *Tarawa*'s maze of narrow steel corridors, bellowing encouragement and mild jibes to almost everyone he encounters.

But here in the room, as he surveys the crisis action team, Moore suddenly scowls and announces the first order of business: figuring out why there are too damned many people in the room. Unlike most organizations, the Marines tend to inversely correlate the number of people on a task and the likelihood of the task's successful completion. What's more, the presence of every single body beyond the absolutely minimum number required means that some other job isn't getting done as quickly as it could—a key consideration when your organization is trying to accomplish more in two days than most companies would in two months. The only people who should be in the room are those who will play a role in executing the mission plan that is being decided on. (The Marines used to leave mission planning to a group of officers who specialized in it and who would hand the finished mission plans over to the executing officers. But that process, it was decided, not only was too time-consuming but left the Marines who carried out the missions with less background information to fall back on when the plans went awry.)

This evening the overpopulation problem is solved, albeit after a little good-natured grumbling, when Moore discovers that a writer and his Marine escort are sitting in as observers. Moore is further placated when he's told that the psychological operations specialist— a sort of director of propaganda—has been purposely left out of the meeting because there isn't much need to persuade or frighten the local population when you're there to feed them. In fact an additional dozen or so officers are taking part in the meeting "virtually":

the meeting is being broadcast as a videoconference to similar rooms in the two other ships attached to the MEU.

Despite the fact that the team has been pared down to the bare minimum, no one in the group is indispensable to the process. There is enough redundancy in responsibility in the MEU that a substitute could stand in for any one of the officers at a moment's notice. Even Moore could be replaced, by his executive officer. Not only does this policy prevent planning gaps, or even paralysis, when a contributor is taken out of the picture, but it also allows around-the-clock planning, with substitutes filling in whenever someone from the main team needs to rest. The officer appointed the "battle-watch captain" (normally a major, but in a MEU the term is applied regardless of rank) is responsible for coordinating the various hand-offs and overlaps between planning groups.

Whatever mission the Marines put together in response to this mission order, they have three hours to plan it and three hours to prepare for it. If they're lucky, they'll get a few hours of sleep before they have to execute it. There is little wasted time. Since the group knew that sooner or later it would have a mission like this, it could have met earlier to plan at a more relaxed pace, then waited for the order to come in. But Marines don't like to plan too far ahead of time, or in the absence of clear orders: an unexpected twist to the orders or new developments in the situation onshore might make the earlier planning irrelevant. As Moore puts it: "Plan early, plan twice." (There are always exceptions. Some flight missions, for example, need to be planned further ahead of time because of the complexities that can be involved in lining up air corridors.)

But even if speedy decision-making weren't strictly necessary, Moore would demand it anyway. In environments where conditions can quickly flip and where the opposition can regroup and take the advantage in a heartbeat, the Marines consider indecisiveness a fatal flaw—worse than making a mediocre decision, because a mediocre decision, especially if swiftly rendered and executed, at least stands a chance. In planning missions, as well as in almost everything else, the point is constantly brought home to Marines that fast and bold is where it's at.

Driven by the notion that there is a cost to every minute spent mulling over decisions, the Marines have worked to push as much inefficiency as possible out of the mission-planning process. "If your decision-making loop is more streamlined than your enemy's, then you set the pace and course of the battle," says Major General John Admire, who commands an infantry division at Camp Pendleton.

The drawback to fast decisionmaking, of course, is that the decision may have to be rendered while information is still sketchy or not yet filtered and analyzed. This fact leads to a sort of organizational uncertainty principle: the faster your decision-making cycle, the less assurance you can have that you're making the best possible decision. "If you're going to have a higher tempo than the enemy, you have to accept a higher degree of uncertainty," says one colonel, adding that there can be a benefit to the uncertainty: it leads to breaking challenges down into more manageable chunks. "If you strive for low uncertainty, you'll have a longer decision-making process that is more likely to be driven to big win-or-lose decisions," he explains. "Small, frequent, rapid decisions will save you from having to come up with a big decision at the eleventh hour."

Still, making quick decisions in the face of incomplete, uncertain, or undigested information is not easy, and it's especially discomfiting when you know that a mistake could cost you your own life and the lives of your colleagues. But Marines get used to it, says Moore. "Everyone is always looking for perfect truth, but you never have it," he says. "Even if you did have it, the other guy is up to something, so by the time you execute it your truth isn't perfect anymore."

For all these reasons, Marines speak of the "70 percent solution," by which they mean an imperfect decision whose saving grace is that it can be made right now.

PRINCIPLE #1: AIM FOR THE 70 PERCENT SOLUTION

By promoting the 70 percent solution, Marines do not advocate shoot-from-the-hip decision-making. Neither do they condone fast, foolish plans. But they do caution against waiting until all the angles are figured out. Instead, when time is of the essence, Marines act as soon as they have a plan with a good chance of working.

FAST VERSUS PERFECT

Former Marine Robert Lutz's signature strategy, first at Ford of Europe and then later at Chrysler, was a form of 70 percent solution: quickly pushing into production bold designs that garnered high praise along with a certain amount of harsh criticism. Ford's imported Merkur in the late 1980s was one Lutz effort that didn't catch on with the market (though to this day it maintains an enthusiastic base of fans), but Chrysler's Viper was a huge hit. The best example of an automotive 70 percent solution may turn out to be the new DaimlerChrysler PT Cruiser. Though Lutz left the company before its introduction, preproduction focus groups indicated that about 65 percent of those people who had strong reactions to the car loved it, and the rest hated it.

In contrast, consider Purple Moon, a much-hyped software game vendor that spent four years and millions of dollars researching young girls' interests as part of a painfully slow effort to bring out what were supposed to be can't-miss products. Despite huge leaps in the market for software games oriented to girls—a 38 percent jump in 1998 alone—the products flopped, and the company ceased operations in 1999.

SITUATIONAL ESSENCE

Moore asks that the mission order as received from divisional command be thrown up on the video projection screen at the far end of the room. (The images are simultaneously transmitted to the videoconference attendees.) The projector is hooked up to a laptop on which the order and several other virtual "slides" have been prepared and loaded. A young Marine mans the keyboard, selecting the slides and creating new ones to reflect the meeting's progress.

Moore asks for a statement of the order's "essence"—that is, for the order to be reworded in the clearest, most succinct, and most relevant terms possible. The group decides that the essence of the order is to provide food and medical aid to a starving and sick population.

One of the Marines' greatest tools is simplicity: taking complex, confusing, or ambiguous situations and concepts and boiling them down to their essence. An essence may lose some of the subtleties, and it may even entirely ignore points that from the point of view of some observers would be important. But the key to an essence is that it portrays a situation or order in a way that is easily grasped and actionable. A simple example—when a Marine commander orders that communications be established, the unit doesn't have to wonder about what sort of communications the commander has in mind. To a Marine, "establishing communications" is shorthand for "getting in touch with those units that can support us on our mission, or that we can support." Any other communications can wait. Obtaining or providing support thus becomes the essence of communications.

PRINCIPLE #2: FIND THE ESSENCE

Sometimes finding the essence of an order involves entertaining ideas that weren't explicit in the original order. When Major General Emil "Buck" Bedard led his Marines into Somalia, he was given orders to "restore normalcy to the cities." The orders did not elaborate on what "normalcy" might entail. "I asked, 'What's normal about U.S. cities?'" recalls Bedard. "Then we decided: normalcy means people are in their homes, there isn't much violence in the streets, the kids are in school, and commerce is taking place." This description of normalcy then became the essence of the order.

THE HEART OF THE PROCESS

Having found the order's essence, Moore's team now runs through a series of steps, each intended to address a question that needs to be answered before they can decide on a course of action. Here are some of the key questions.

What Are Our Strengths and Weaknesses and What Are Those of the Opponent?

The Marines want to know where they're most likely to run into trouble and where they're likely to be able to leverage a strength. They also want to figure out the same for the enemy so that they can exploit its weaknesses and avoid its best shots.

In a humanitarian mission there often isn't an "enemy," at least in the conventional sense. That's the case tonight, so Moore's group need only identify its own strengths and weaknesses. They determine that their key strength is knowledge of the terrain, and that their greatest weakness is their susceptibility to the disease that has felled much of the local population. With these points identified, the group can, for example, pick base locations that minimize exposure to insects.

In general, the Marines try to avoid coming up with long lists when answering important questions, lest they end up with so many things to worry about that they can't effectively deal with the most important ones. Instead, they tend to limit their focus to the three most important elements. (The choice of the number-three priority, as discussed later on, is not an arbitrary one, and it arises over and over again in many different contexts.)

What Assumptions Can We Make?

In high-speed planning there is almost always a shortage of clear, complete, certain information about threats and opportunities. It would be safest simply to assume the worst about every element of the mission. But having to think about and prepare for every possible negative contingency would be paralyzing. Instead, the Marines at least eliminate from attention those conditions that seem highly unlikely and take as givens those conditions that seem very probable. In fact most people make these sorts of assumptions when considering courses of action. But the Marines like to spell these assumptions out, as a way of ensuring that the entire team is making the same ones. Moore's group, for example, makes explicit the assumption that they will not be threatened by nuclear, biological, or chemical weapons or by land mines.

What Must We Not Do?

Decision-makers who are perfectly clear on what they need to accomplish sometimes fail to consider the unintended consequences of their actions—consequences whose harm can outweigh whatever good the mission accomplishes. In other words, determining what actions must be avoided can sometimes be at least as important as deciding on the actions that must be taken. Sometimes these unacceptable actions are implicit in the orders, but if so, they need to be made explicit during this session. Tonight Moore's team decides that damaging property would be unacceptable, since it could lead to a loss of popular support for the Marines' efforts and make it difficult to distribute food safely.

How Will the Mission Affect Morale?

The best-planned mission can fall apart if the people executing it lose faith in it or become discouraged by conditions. Marine decision-makers always keep the attitudes of their people in mind. Moore's group does not anticipate serious problems with regard to morale. Humanitarian missions tend to be uplifting, and in this case there's no reason to expect the hostile reactions from the local population that can make aid-givers question their purpose.

What Are Our "Bump" Plans?

Being convinced that nothing can go wrong is an open invitation for everything to go wrong. The Marines always have at least one fall-back plan—a "bump" plan—in mind. For this mission the bump plan is simply to pull back to the base camp and defend it if unexpected hostilities are encountered.

What Are We Overlooking?

Now that possible plans are starting to take shape as these questions are answered, it's time to wonder whether some angles are being missed. The Marines hold it as an article of faith that something is being overlooked and take the time to brainstorm about what it is. According to Moore, one mission nearly failed in the last MEU full-scale exercise because the execution team didn't take along enough spare batteries to keep special communications equipment powered up.

Tonight Moore's group has been gravitating toward a plan to hand out some of the MEU's own large store of MREs (meals ready to eat) as a stopgap measure to help the starving population until more food supplies arrive. But one officer points out that the somewhat rich MREs could easily overwhelm the digestive system of a person suffering from severe malnutrition. Another notes that the MREs may be incompatible with some of the population's ethnic and religious dietary restrictions.

CULTURE CHECK

Justice Technology offers an offbeat example of how easy it is to overlook potential problems when dealing with an unfamiliar culture, as so many businesses are doing in an increasingly global economy. Justice is a phone service provider that was founded by two people in 1992 and has since rocketed to revenues of $57 million, parlaying success in a minuscule niche market to virtual domination of certain segments of the global phone business. When Justice offered international phone service to corporate customers in Argentina, it highlighted the savings it was bringing to the companies by detailing the discount of each call on the monthly bill. But though customers were impressed by the savings, many were horrified that the calls were detailed at all—this standard feature of U.S. phone bills was a novelty in Argentina. Nonplussed that customers would complain about having their calls broken out, CEO David Glickman learned that many Argentine businessmen keep Swiss bank accounts that they would just as soon not advertise to the government through phone bills that list calls to Switzerland. Others expressed concern about their wives discovering multiple calls to certain numbers. And one oddly secretive company wasn't pleased to see that its bills revealed that 90 percent of its calls went to Iran and Nicaragua, two countries that had little in common other than their great interest to the American intelligence community. "We could have made a lot of money charging people to not have call detail on their bills," says Glickman.

MOVING TO A DECISION

Now in the final round of the process, the team takes steps to translate its thinking into actionable concepts.

Obtain Clarification
Some of the issues raised during the session require more information from headquarters. For example, is the MEU supposed to provide a range of medical treatment or just enough to keep the sickest people alive ("to give them Band-Aids and watch them bleed," as one officer puts it)? When will more food be shipped to them? Should they worry about giving out too much food, taking the risk that the population will abandon their farms and become dependent on the aid? Are the rains that produced the flooding likely to continue? The Marines aren't so proud of their independence that

they're ashamed to ask key questions like these. What would be shameful, however, would be not taking action in the absence of answers, which could be a long time in coming. Thus, Moore's group isn't going to wait; in just one hour the group needs to start drawing up the detailed plans of the mission on which it has decided. If and when the answers from headquarters eventually come in, the MEU will adjust its missions on the fly to reflect them.

Describe the Goal

The group, now close to the end of the process, is ready to phrase the mission goal, in the form of a reasonable and measurably achievable situation that reflects their capabilities and understanding of the obstacles. (As we see in a later chapter, the Marines refer to such goals as "end states" and make them a central part of their management philosophy.) The goal they agree on is to get MREs into the hands of as many starving people as possible and to provide at least minimal medical aid to the sickest members of the population until better food and medical aid arrives. True, the MREs are less than ideal as food aid for a malnourished population, and the medical aid will be inadequate—but both forms of aid are better than nothing, and there's good reason to believe that better resources will soon become available. It's a true 70 percent solution.

Propose Possible Mission Plans

Having specified a goal, the group's last responsibility is to propose three alternative missions that might achieve the goal. Not yet detailed are questions such as which Marines should go, how many, where they should go, and how they should get there. Normally the team favors one mission but attempts to come up with two alternatives, if for no other reason than to stimulate thinking and perhaps highlight an angle that's been overlooked. (As we see later on, the addition of two alternatives is in keeping with a Marine predilection for managing in groups of three. But the predilection isn't meant to be an overly restrictive rule. As Brigadier General Stephen Johnson puts it: "If you've got six great ideas, then go ahead and throw them in. And if you can't think of a third decent idea, then don't add one as eyewash.")

Decide, Then Invite Dissent

The final choice between the three is Moore's, but generally the top decisionmaker will go along with the team if there's a clear favorite. If he or she chooses one of the alternatives, however, that decision is not necessarily taken as gospel. Marine decision-makers not only allow disagreement at this stage but practically demand that every key member of the staff try to shoot holes in the decision, taking yet another opportunity to catch something that everyone has missed. Tonight, when the smoke clears, Moore's decision stands, and he prepares to end the meeting to let the officers get started on working out the mission details. But first he asks the group for "saved rounds." Saved rounds are the rounds of ammunition issued to soldiers before a mission or practice shoot that must be collected after it's over because they remained unspent. Figuratively the term refers to unvoiced comments, especially those representing disagreement or concern. It's the last chance for anyone who has doubts to speak his or her mind.

FOLLOW-UP

Executives who come up with brilliant plans are sometimes at a loss to explain why the plans failed in execution. Marines know the reason may not be that the mission orders were flawed, or that the people involved weren't up to carrying them out, but rather that the orders weren't clearly communicated all the way down the chain to the frontline people. Orders can be mistranslated at each step, as in a game of telephone.

To erase any such misunderstandings, Marines run through a "final mission brief" before kicking off the execution of the mission. Normally present at the brief are the high-level officers who directed the decision-making and the midlevel officers who worked out the mission details. Often the enlisted officers who will be doing the hands-on direction of the frontline Marines are included, too. In fact nowadays enlisted officers are being brought higher and higher up into the planning process. "Under the old system the sergeant found out what was going on when it was time to get ready to leave on the mission," says Randy Gangle, a retired Marine colonel who now consults to the Corps. "Now he's often in on the meeting that takes place ten hours before that, so he can start his planning, get his people rested, and prepare the ammo."

The briefing is typically given by midlevel officers, each of whom presents the details of his or her own piece of the mission. The goal isn't to reconsider the decisions that have been made; once the saved rounds are collected and the decisions converted into orders, Marines try to leave their minds untroubled by questions about the orders themselves and instead focus on carrying them out. The point of the final briefing is simply to make sure each person understands what everyone else is doing. "You're looking for nodding heads," says Colonel Rick Zilmer. "The first time you see someone's head going from side to side, you stop."

No matter how carefully the mission orders were decided on and planned out, Marines recognize that once the mission gets going there is a good chance that it will have to deviate from the original plans. Things go wrong; new information comes in; the opposition behaves in a surprising way. "Whatever plan you devise, it probably isn't going to come out that way," says retired Major General O. K. Steele. Armed with a mission end state and the commander's intent, the Marines executing the mission are capable of improvising. Over the longer term, however, commanders need to be able to amend missions and come up with new ones to reflect the situation in the field.

But judging the situation can be a challenge in its own right. That's why, whenever possible, Marines try to come up with quantifiable parameters for keeping tabs on mission success—even when the mission deals with something as hard to quantify as a population's state of mind. In Somalia, Bedard wanted to keep track of the Marines' success in "restoring normalcy" to the cities. "How do you figure out if you're doing better in a chaotic situation like that?" he says. His team came up with the following benchmarks: the percentage of huts into which families had moved back; the number of people in feeding lines; the number of people showing up at hospital emergency rooms with bullet wounds; the number of students at school; the number of lanterns lit at night; the number of local police on duty; and the percentage of women wearing jewelry to the market—the custom before the breakdown in law and order had made it risky. Every day Bedard reviewed estimates of each of these counts. As the bullet wound counts dropped and others rose, Bedard knew the mission was on track.

Now that we have a sense of the speed and flexibility with which the Marines operate, let's take a look in the next chapter at how the Corps defines its role as an organization.

☆ ☆ ☆ ☆ ☆

2. MISSION

We do windows.

—USMC COLONEL (RET.) JAMES LASSWELL

As we saw in the last chapter, Marines are prepared to undertake a staggering array of missions, from friendly humanitarian aid to tense police actions to out-and-out vicious combat. It's reasonable to ask a basic question: What are the Marines for exactly? Anyone can identify the primary jobs of the Army, the Navy, or the Air Force. But what do the Marines do that justifies the Corps as a separate service?

There are, of course, certain types of missions that have become almost exclusively associated with Marines: beach invasions and the evacuation of Americans from hostile environments overseas are two obvious examples. But in fact the Army has long been capable of beach invasions; the D-Day Normandy landing, for example, was an Army operation. And all three of the larger services are capable of quickly inserting highly trained soldiers into hostile environments to lead civilians to safety.

In truth, there is little the Marine Corps does that couldn't be seen as redundant with the services performed by the other branches of the military. Nevertheless, the occasional tentative feelers around Washington about absorbing the Corps into the Army are invariably quashed as soon as they are tendered. The reason: the Marine Corps is invaluable not because the other services can't perform its assignments, but because the Marines complete them faster and more effectively. It is this speed and impact over a wide range of missions, rather than the missions themselves, that define the Marines Corps.

The Marines have concentrated on building certain types of generic expertise and skills without restricting themselves to applying them in particular ways. By distinguishing itself not by what it provides but by the style in which it operates, the Corps has maintained a strong sense of focus and a clear picture of the people, practices, and resources it needs, without narrowing its purpose. Along the way, the Marines have rethought the very meaning of organizational mission.

SHIFTING FOCUS

Organizations have always been defined by the products or services they deliver, especially in the business world. General Motors was a car manufacturer. Compaq was a personal computer manufacturer. Brooklyn Gas was a gas and electric utility. But more and more companies, finding themselves hit hard by competition in their core industries but also surrounded by outside opportunities, are pushing into new businesses. Thus, GM, using its experience in car financing, has become a giant in consumer lending. Compaq, with its mastery of large corporate account management, is moving into software and networking support and services. Brooklyn Gas had acquired information technology expertise to track customer transactions and is now using it in the data communications business. Thus, the definitions of what these companies are about has started to blur.

Today organizations that remain defined by a product may risk sudden disaster. Netscape's founder, James Clark, has said that the biggest mistake his company made was to remain too enamored of what it thought of as its flagship product, the Navigator browser software. By the time Netscape's management recognized that the real value of the company had shifted away from software and toward its website, the firm was already in trouble. No company is immune: by 1999 Levi Strauss, owner of what had been for over a century one of the world's most highly regarded products and brand names, had seen its jeans fall out of favor, dragging the value of the brand down with them and forcing the company into its first major round of layoffs.

BEING CAPABILITY-BASED
RATHER THAN THREAT-BASED

Organizations risk placing themselves at a disadvantage when they allow themselves to become defined by what they do, rather than by how they do it, because the environment in which almost everyone operates today has become extraordinarily dynamic.

Few organizations have been harder hit by the transformation of once-static environments into ultradynamic ones than the U.S. Army. For nearly half a century the Army focused the vast majority of its planning and resources on being prepared to face the gigantic, well-equipped, highly trained, and monolithic military forces of the Soviet Union and its Eastern Bloc allies. It was an entirely appropriate course in view of the challenges of the Cold War. But suddenly, with the fall of communism, the threat changed: now the enemy could be any of dozens of small countries, or factions within countries, and the conflict is more likely to be a relatively constrained set of battles, or even a police action, than all-out war. This is not to say that the Army isn't equipped to handle such conflicts; as the conflict in Yugoslavia illustrates, however, it has not been set up to handle them quickly, and painful gaps and inefficiencies too often result.

In Marine terms, the Army became "threat-based" during the Cold War. That is, it shaped itself on the assumption that it had a clearly identified set of competitors who could be expected to behave in conflict in a fairly understandable fashion. When the threat changed, the Army became less effective.

In contrast, the Marines have become a "capability-based" organization. They have resisted the temptation to become especially relevant to a particular set of competitors in a particular environment, and thus they have avoided the risk of becoming less relevant in others. As the competitive environment changes, the Marines simply find new ways to apply the impressive generic capabilities they have achieved. The Corps has made it clear that it can and will take on any assignment the nation sees fit to assign to it, no questions asked. This is not an idle boast: from October 1997 to October 1998, the Marines were called in to no less than twenty-two military, protection, and humanitarian assistance operations around the world.

Given this sort of range, it might be easy to misread the Marines as unfocused. But in fact the Marines have a clear organizational mission, one tied to its capabilities rather than to the types of operations it handles. That mission? To be a major combat force that reacts faster, hits harder, and is more versatile and familiar with complexity than any other major combat force in the world.

PRINCIPLE #3: BUILD A CAPABILITY-BASED ORGANIZATIONAL MISSION

Note that the Marines haven't limited themselves to a single competency. Instead, they have laid out a set of competency goals, with two common themes: they aim for the competencies that are the most difficult for combat forces to master, and the competencies that are typically required by the most challenging military assignments. We discuss in later chapters exactly how the Marines achieve these competencies. For now suffice it to say that, by achieving them, the Marines virtually guarantee that their services will remain in demand and that they will prevail in their individual missions.

THE TWO UNIVERSALLY CRITICAL COMPETENCIES

Second Marine Division Commanding Major General Bedard, a man who looks like an oversized fireplug mounted with a cannonball chiseled into a face inspired by Popeye's, recounts in his gruff, booming voice how he was sitting down with his wife to his wedding anniversary dinner at their home in Camp Pendleton near San Diego when he got the phone call alerting him to Iraq's invasion of Kuwait. "You'd do anything to get out of our anniversary dinner, wouldn't you?" he recalls his wife saying when he told her the news. Fourteen days later Bedard stepped onto Saudi Arabian soil accompanied by a Marine force capable, if necessary, of fighting all the way into Kuwait City. (Ultimately Marine units were indeed the first to enter Kuwait City.)

The Army's "light infantry" divisions consist primarily of troops with guns who can be sent on short notice to hot spots. But Bedard's force was anything but light. It included jets, helicopters, tanks, heavy artillery, and all the supplies and facilities necessary to support thousands of men and their equipment in a small but furious war lasting several weeks. The arrival of the Marines in the Gulf represented a long-distance transfer of full-scale, state-of-the-art fighting power at unprecedented speed.

The Marines have targeted four primary competencies: impact, speed, versatility, and proficiency with complex situations. Though all four represent crucial aspects of the Corps' overall capabilities, two of them—speed and proficiency with complexity—are worth highlighting here. In today's high-competition, fast-changing business environment, it's getting harder and harder to envision a company that can achieve and sustain success without staking out these two competencies.

PRINCIPLE #4: ORIENT TOWARD SPEED AND COMPLEXITY

The Marines are famous for their expeditionary capabilities: the combat-ready forces they keep floating at sea can hit the beaches of almost any nonlandlocked country in the world within a few days of receiving warning orders. And occasionally in less time than that. In 1994 Colonel Richard Barry was commanding one of the Marines' floating forces when word came in that he was to take his unit to Kuwait, in response to an Iraqi buildup at the border. Sixteen hours later CNN was filming Barry's battalion as it set up on a Kuwaiti beach. "We took our combat power in that country from 0 to 100 percent in hours," says Barry. "We heard later that Saddam was watching CNN at the time, and he turned to his minister of defense and asked, 'Where did those guys come from?'"

Things don't slow down once the Marines take the beach. In 1992 Bedard had been yanked from Thanksgiving dinner at his home to command the Marine forces heading for famine-stricken Somalia. After the Marines landed, they headed directly inland, and in 30 hours they had made their way 280 miles to the city of Baidoa, at the heart of the famine, traveling most of the way not only without paved roads but often without even trails, in 112-degree heat. Some 1,500 Marines were soon distributing the 15 tons of Australian wheat they had trucked in with them.

Another example: in 1996, concerned that the United States did not have effective capabilities in place for dealing with the aftermath of a massive biochemical disaster, Congress turned to the Marines. Planning a national disaster response force, and training and equipping people for it, could reasonably have taken years. The Marines were ready in six months.

The Marines have maintained their vaunted position in the military largely because they've made it their business to leave everyone else in their dust when it comes to response time and pace. Any organization that makes far-faster-than-average speed its hallmark—without unduly sacrificing competence, of course—has won a critical competitive edge over competition.

The same is true of becoming adept at dealing with complex situations. Complexity can emerge from a number of factors: the need to accomplish simultaneous and multiple missions; a shortage of information (or equally disabling, a glut of raw information); situational novelty; situational ambiguity; multiple threats or obstacles; and, most challenging of all, rapidly changing conditions. In Haiti and Somalia the Marines faced every one of these conditions. Mobs could form almost anywhere, at any time. Killers mingled in crowds of innocent civilians. Alliances and conflicts within the population sprang up and fell apart hour by hour. The Marines had to fight, police, and feed people at the same time at several different places.

THE SUPERCHARGED CORPORATION

Speed has always been useful in the business world, but over the past decade it has become essential, and for a simple reason: almost everything else has sped up. Organizations that operate at a less-than-whirlwind pace risk being left behind. In some industries—especially the technology-oriented and financial services sectors—windows of opportunity open and shut in months, and sometimes in weeks or even days. The management consultant George Stalk Jr. has said that speeding up a business used to provide a 20 to 30 percent improvement in performance, but that "when you move into the digital world, you attach a supercharger to speed as a competitive weapon."

One company caught briefly napping was Ericsson, which after achieving spectacular success in the cell-phone market saw its share of U.S. sales of digital phones cut in half in 1998 because it had been slow to adapt to a new type of transmission technology that suddenly became popular with cell-phone service providers. General Electric, on the other hand, has been determined to stay in front of an emerging shift toward conducting many business-to-business transactions over the Web. Its Polymerland subsidiary now monitors some customers' inventories of Polymerland products and issues orders to replenish them, all automatically, over the Web. The subsidiary has been on track to increase the number of its transactions conducted over the Web from 5 percent to 50 percent—in one year.

VeriFone, a vendor of credit-card verification and other electronic payment systems, had revenues of nearly $500 million a year when it was bought by Hewlett-Packard in 1997. In the late 1980s, before the vast majority of companies had even discovered e-mail, VeriFone was conducting virtually all its internal business online between employees scattered around the globe and had found ways to apply this capability to gain an edge in speed over competitors. Imagine the surprise of the Greek bank executives who asked a VeriFone rep late one day for customer references on a debit-card system when the rep show up first thing the next morning, looking crisp and wielding a customized report the size of a small phone book detailing the experiences of nearly one hundred businesses with the system. The evening before the rep had fired off an e-mail to colleagues asking for assistance, and VeriFone employees around the world pitched in to create the report, passing the report to various offices in different time zones so that the work literally followed the sun around the globe. Employees had even enlisted the help of a team of outside translators to render the final report in Greek. The stunned bank executives signed that day.

Many industries have become hotbeds of shifting alliances and competition, with goals that change from week to week. There used to be a simple means of keeping score: profits. Now businesses fight madly across the globe over everything from market share to distribution channels to telecommunications bandwidth, often ignoring mounting losses. Wall Street is no longer even sure how to put a rough value on some companies. Who could doubt that organizations adept at fast-changing, confusing conditions are far more likely to prevail?

AN EXERCISE IN CONFUSION

To get some sense of the complex and fast-changing nature of the environments faced by the Marine Corps—and of how determined the Marines are to master these environments—let's follow a Marine through a simulated mission provided by an experimental combat squad leader's course run at Camp Pendleton. A squad is running a patrol—that is, moving through an unsecured area where there may be an enemy threat. The patrol is considered one of the most fundamental of all Marine missions, but as this partially computerized simulation makes clear, it can also be a phenomenally confusing, stressful, and altogether challenging experience for the patrol leader.

The simulation takes place in a large, darkened room with a computer-projection screen at one end and desks crowded with computer and electronic equipment at the other, manned by a few technicians and the person running the simulation, Bing West, a former Marine colonel and now a civilian contractor. On the day I observe, a rangy sergeant in his midtwenties stands in front of the screen, wearing a radio headset, as he normally might on a patrol. All the information that goes through his radio is being spoken by West and is broadcast through a loudspeaker so that everyone in the room can hear what's going on.

West gives the sergeant, whose code name is Blade, a pre-patrol briefing similar to one a lieutenant would give his or her squad leaders. Blade's squad will be split into four patrols that will move through the "092 grid square," referring to a map projected on the screen. "The temperature is eighty degrees, with intense humidity," says West. "You can call in air or artillery. There are civilians in need, but some are enemy sympathizers, and there have been ambushes. You need to clear the sector of threats. Avoid civilian casualties and collateral damage. Remember, Blade, we're here to help these people."

Blade begins by choosing the gear for his squad, selecting from a wide range of weapons, ammunition, food, water, and miscellaneous gear, such as night-vision goggles and smoke markers. He can take anything he wants, but the weight per squad member climbs with every additional item, and too much weight could come back to haunt Blade in the form of a prematurely fatigued squad—a development that the simulation would duly track. After turning down a laser-target-designator, Blade declares himself good to go, having given his squad forty-five pounds each to hump.

Blade indicates through his radio where he wants his patrol to head on the map, and the screen displays a view through the eyes of someone making his way down the streets of a Third World city. Within seconds Blade picks up an urgent radio call from one of the other squads: "Blade, Blade, refugees are streaming at us, there are over a hundred of them. We're giving them our water. What should we do? What should we say?" (This voice, and most of the others, are provided by West, who is not entirely talentless as a character actor.) Blade responds immediately: "Negative on the water. Do *not* give them your water." Blade has provided his squad with just enough water for the patrol, hoping to hold weight down. He directs the besieged patrol away from the refugees.

Moments later another call for instructions comes in: a patrol has run into a band of looters, and the corporal running that team asks Blade for permission to fire over their heads, "or maybe give them a couple of butt strokes." Blade says no—just keep an eye on them. The corporal, sounding highly agitated now, shouts that the looters are surrounding the patrol and that some are spitting on them. Blade orders the corporal to have his squad fix bayonets and move away from the crowd. "If they get close enough to grab your weapons, take action," he adds. Before that situation is resolved, another patrol radios in: a sniper is picking at them from a building to the north, but he's reported to be "a lousy shot." Then the voice becomes wild: a Marine named Jones is down, hit by the sniper; the rest of the patrol is pinned down around the corner by more gunfire. Blade doesn't hesitate: "Get Jones," he says firmly. Then he calls for a medivac chopper.

Soon Blade's patrol is involved in a firefight outside a church. Blade eventually calls in artillery and F-18 strikes. As often happens in real life, he forgets to move one of his patrols out of the area that is to be struck, but West has one of his characters give Blade a friendly (and realistic) reminder, rather than allowing the sergeant to decimate part of his own squad. Several more encounters with the local population ensue. Eventually the biggest problem will be a shortage of water. Almost every Marine who runs through this simulation underestimates how much water an active person will run through on a long, hot, humid day.

Later Blade is given a second mission. The squad is to secure a bridge, taking care not to bring harm to a nearby museum containing some $400 million worth of Picassos. "Picasso is a famous artist," West adds, Marines never being ones to assume anything when giving orders. West also warns Blade that a large enemy force was sighted in the area earlier in the day, and he tells Blade to avoid ending up outgunned, though the area appears to be clear now, he adds. "This is really an easy one," says West—a tip-off that everything will go wrong.

Sure enough, the squad is soon trapped on the bridge, taking fire from the large enemy force, which is positioned between the bridge and the museum. The only help available is a gun on a Navy ship several miles away. Naval guns are notoriously imprecise, but Blade recognizes that his squad's lives probably depend on calling in that fire. He calls in the fire. The enemy is taken out—along with the Picassos.

Later West notes that the key to this second mission is to move back as soon as the enemy is seen, before it can trap the squad. "If the commander's intent is not to get overmatched, then sometimes you have to pull out," he says. "It's an unorthodox Marine tactic, but sometimes it's the right thing." The other lesson: try not to rely on Navy guns when accuracy counts.

On a more general level, says West, the course is meant to help squad leaders learn how to transform a confusing, often panicky situation into a manageable picture in their own minds. "Ninety percent of combat is not being able to see what's going on, not having any right answers," he says. "But you still have to think tactically and give orders crisply. We want them to be able to give us three sentences in forty seconds. The first sentence is an assessment of the situation—the enemy is trying to pin us down against the river. The second is the goal—we are not going to let that happen. The third is the course of action—Jones, lay down suppressing fire; Smith, flank them on the right. . . ." But the most important goal of the course is to make squad leaders familiar enough with the twists and turns of combat situations that when they're confronted with a crisis in a real mission they won't feel completely surprised. Explains West: "We want them to think to themselves, 'I've seen this situation before.'" (Businesses that want to provide managers with an analogous training experience can turn to software simulators such as "Start-Up" from Montecristo Multimedia, which sends a would-be entrepreneur through a series of realistic financial and management obstacles.)

ADJUSTING THE MISSION

Though the Marines have always emphasized fast reaction and high impact, it is more recently that the Corps has added a focus on mastering complexity and versatility. As a capability-based organization, the Marines have recognized that they have to keep an eye on the changing landscape and reassess the question of which capabilities provide the greatest edge.

The emphasis on complexity, for example, arose from two trends. As discussed earlier, one is the emergence of the confusing, fast-changing, primarily urban missions that mix combat and humanitarian assistance. Another is the American public's shrinking willingness to accept losses of troops in battle. Ever since Vietnam, when television cameras brought the horrors of battle into the country's living rooms and a majority of the public came to question whether the goals of the war justified the casualties, the Marines have understood that winning the battle may not be good enough; the battle also has to be won with far fewer losses than in the past. It is in part this demand that has inspired the Marines to invent new approaches to warfighting based on smaller, highly maneuverable fighting units that strike in unpredictable fashion. The trade-off in the new style of fighting is that it generates patterns of action and reaction that are hard to coordinate—and consequently highly complex.

The Corps' increased emphasis on versatility, on the other hand, has been strengthened not so much out of need as out of opportunity. One key opportunity has been the availability of transport technology that allows the Marines to strike deep inland from ships stationed far off the coast. For most of its existence, the Corps' fast-strike utility was largely restricted to littoral, or near-coastline, missions in which its troops were offloaded from Navy ships a few miles offshore onto eight-mile-per-hour amphibious vehicles or onto helicopters with a fifty-mile range. Now the Marines are fielding amphibious vehicles that can bring troops roaring in at more than fifty miles per hour from ships stationed safely out of sight below the horizon seventeen miles away, and helicopters with ranges of more than five hundred miles. As a result, the Marines can take on a wider variety of missions over a far larger area.

By using new technology and techniques to strike faster and farther from the ocean, the Marines are essentially extending their sphere of usefulness without completely turning their backs on their traditional specialty of littoral attacks. Instead of looking for entirely new lines of work, the Marines have been successful at applying their capability-based approach to extend their old line of work into new missions.

BROADENING REACH

The idea of expanding into new markets in keeping with a skill-based organizational mission is starting to hold sway in the business world, too. Consider how Federal Express, after mastering the use of automation to execute and track package deliveries, has built a secondary business providing warehousing and shipping capabilities to other companies. Likewise, Sony has parlayed its expertise in scoping out the public's tastes and preferences in audio equipment and television to make forays into computers, smart phones, and interactive cable television.

The capabilities on which an organization successfully stakes its competitive edge can be surprising. Consider Griffin Hospital in Derby, Connecticut, where patient satisfaction has soared to 96 percent—an astounding level in any industry, and one that's almost unheard of in the hospital business—and admissions have been rising an average of 2 percent a year over the past four years, with healthy revenues and cash flow, all within competing distance of seven other hospitals, including the world-renowned Yale–New Haven Hospital. Griffin's edge? Niceness. While other hospitals highlight prestigious physicians and state-of-the-art equipment, Griffin has emphasized an empathetic nursing staff, physicians who bring patients into the decision-making, and amenities ranging from music in the parking lot and patient-accessible kitchens in every wing to a twenty-four-hour visiting policy. What's more, Griffin has leveraged its focus on caring by opening up new wards for specialty therapies, including chronic pain management and wound treatment.

Focusing on a capability-based organizational mission rather than a threat-based one is a critical prerequisite to long-term success in a highly competitive and fast-changing environment. But the bigger challenge lies in outdoing the competition when it comes to developing and applying those sought-after capabilities. In the next chapter, we explore one of the key factors underlying the Marines' success in this regard.

☆ ☆ ☆ ☆ ☆

3. STRUCTURE

The nineteen-year-old Marine is now an instrument of national policy.
—KIRK NICHOLAS, MARINE COMBAT DEVELOPMENT GROUP

Colonel Robert Schmidle has spent the night watching Marines battle over a small American town. The town is the one that makes up the heart of Camp Lejeune in North Carolina, and for two days it has been standing in for a third-world city. The scenario: the insurgent "Landrones," aided by a number of army regulars from neighboring "Redesia"—all played by Marines—are controlling the city, and the Marines have landed to take the city back. The battle has been hard-fought but bloodless: "kills" have been achieved with low-power laser beams rather than bullets or shells. Aside from that all-important distinction, the combat has been realistic in every way. The buildings through which the fighting has raged are actual apartment complexes, office buildings, and malls. A post office, a dental clinic, and even a church—rumor had it that a wedding was taking place when the invasion struck—have all been targeted for search-and-destroy missions. Throughout the night amphibious assault vehicles, tanks, helicopters, and an endless stream of heavily armed Marines have raced around the town exchanging bursts of fire, radios crackling nonstop.

Now it's 8:00 A.M., and though Schmidle hasn't slept in about twenty-six hours, he seems hyper-awake and eager to rehash some of the night's key events. For instance: "Our helicopters were spreading out when a shaky intelligence report came in: the Landrone leader may have been spotted hiding out in a building. The lieutenant who took the report was supposed to be setting up a defense around one of the buildings we had taken. But when he saw the report, and couldn't raise a captain on the radio, he took his men, commandeered two platoons from other companies, and stormed the building the leader was supposedly spotted in. It turned out the intelligence report was wrong. There were only civilians in there."

Like a district attorney shaping an indictment, Schmidle ticks off the salient features of the episode. The lieutenant acted hastily. He acted on shaky and incomplete information. He acted without the express authorization of his commander. He turned his back on his assignment. He pulled other Marines who did not report to him off of their assignments. He scared innocent civilians. And he came away with nothing to show for it.

Schmidle's final assessment: a job well done. "It was a good bet," he says. "The lieutenant did exactly the right thing." In fact the elements of the lieutenant's performance that, translated to the business world, would have gotten him fired in the vast majority of corporations, reflect the very qualities that draw admiration from Schmidle. The Corps is trying to instill those qualities not only in every officer but in every Marine.

In business, decentralization and organizational flattening typically involve gutting several layers of management, and managers are often left overwhelmed with as many as two dozen direct subordinates. The Marines, on the other hand, have pushed down decision-making authority while retaining a simple hierarchical structure designed to keep everyone's job manageable.

Organizations function efficiently when there is a clear-cut chain of command. But in extremely dynamic and complex environments where competitive skirmishes are taking place unpredictably on different fronts and in different forms, the decision-making chain can be fatally slow. By the time information has been passed up from the people at the front lines—be they infantrymen or salespeople—chewed over by higher levels of the chain, and then passed back down as decisions, opportunities are gone, crises have escalated, and subtleties have been lost.

The Marine Corps answer to the problem: encourage the people on the front lines, when pressed for time, to ignore the hierarchy and make decisions outside the loop.

The Marine Corps has a long tradition of distributing battlefield authority to its lowest-level management, embodied by corporals, sergeants, and lieutenants. That commitment to bottom-up thinking has evolved gradually and naturally over the Corps' existence, and for a simple reason: high-risk, high-speed, high-focus assaults tend to be unforgiving on bureaucratic or autocratic management styles. Commanders who refuse to distribute decision-making power to their men quickly find themselves with few men left to command.

In recent years the Corps has vastly stepped up its efforts to push authority out to the field, taking it to levels unheard of in the military and in most organizations of any type. Increasingly even the very lowest ranks of the Marines possess the confidence to act quickly and boldly on their own, even in—*especially* in—situations where the information is scattered and unreliable and their actions could have serious repercussions.

Needless to say, the Marine Corps is not promoting reckless and hasty action on the part of its least-experienced members. Rather, it tries to give its troops the knowledge and experience they need to assess confusing and rapidly evolving situations, weigh alternative plans and their potential consequences, and then do what needs to be done, assigning themselves the authority and resources they need to pull it off as they go. There's no way around it, insist the Marines, if the Corps is going to be prepared to produce ever-faster and more effective responses to an ever-wider range of unpredictable scenarios.

FORMAL HIERARCHY

The Marines are far from hierarchy-free. Hierarchy is regarded by the Corps as essential to smooth and efficient functioning, particularly with regard to making the best possible decisions, coordinating the actions of different parts of the organization, and planning effectively. But the Marines' organizational structure is distinguished by the fact that it operates with two distinctly different hierarchical styles and switches quickly and seamlessly between them as the situation demands.

The first hierarchy—the one the Marines employ to deal with the relatively slow-moving situations typically found in peacetime—is a fairly flat one that most closely resembles the structure of a typical business. During these quiet times between missions, when Marines can focus on administrative and routine maintenance duties, higher-level officers typically find themselves directing staffs of as many as fifteen people.

But when the Marines have a time-critical mission to accomplish, the hierarchy is immediately narrowed, in accordance with a simple scheme: the rule of three. In a nutshell, the rule of three dictates that each Marine has three things to worry about. In terms of organizational structure, a corporal has a squad of three men; a sergeant and second lieutenant have a platoon of three squads; a captain has a company of three platoons; and so on, up to generals.

PRINCIPLE #5: ORGANIZE ACCORDING TO THE RULE OF THREE

The rule of three can be widely applied even outside of management structure. It dictates, for example, that a person should limit his or her attention to three tasks or goals. Applied to decision-making, it prescribes boiling a world of infinite possibilities down to three alternative courses of action. Almost by definition, any Marine who has more than three elements on his or her plate during a mission is overextended and confused. (The Marines didn't pick the number three out of a hat; they've experimented with a rule of four, which proved too slow, and a rule of two, which proved too inefficient.)

Of course, the rule-of-three hierarchy leads to an organizational hierarchy that might strike some businesses as appallingly narrow and tall—there are typically eight full layers of management in between an infantry private and the colonel commanding his unit. That sounds like exactly the sort of stovepipe structure that businesses have been moving away from because of how slowly information and decisions filter up and down. But the Marines have made a critical modification in this structure that allows it to become far faster and more effective than any flattened or networked organizational structure: pushing as much decision-making authority down to lower levels as the situation demands.

Before we examine this "authority on demand" scheme, let's consider the context in which it evolved.

MANEUVERABILITY

The Marines have instituted profound changes in their basic approach to warfighting. Up until the 1960s the Marine Corps relied on the same basic style of fighting used by most modern infantries: a "linear warfare" approach in which two companies of soldiers rush at the enemy while one hangs back to support them. The three platoon leaders (lieutenants) within each company stay in close radio contact with the company commander (a captain), and within each platoon the three squads generally stay within one hundred yards or less of one another so that the squad leaders (sergeants or corporals) can exchange hand signals. In this way, most soldiers can easily keep track of where they are in relation to each other and to the enemy, and commands from company or even battalion leaders can easily be relayed to the troops. Indeed, a battalion commander (colonel) with a good vantage point and daylight often can precisely control the movements of his troops because he can visually track their progress.

In the intense Pacific island fighting of World War II, linear warfare as practiced by fierce, do-or-die Marines was effective, but it also resulted in devastating losses not only for the enemy but also for the victorious Marines. The heavy punishment wreaked by the enemy on the frontally advancing Marines led many observers and critics to refer to their linear style of fighting as "attrition warfare": achieving victory in part by virtue of their ability to replace their dead and wounded more steadily than the enemy could. In the ninety-day battle for Okinawa, virtually every single Marine who was present for the initial weeks of the fighting was killed, wounded, or missing in action.

Starting in the 1960s the Marines began to reinvent the logic of combat. The result was a new style of fighting that became known as "maneuver warfare": rather than swarms of soldiers attacking the enemy directly, smaller groups of soldiers surprise and confuse the enemy by attacking quickly, repeatedly, and unpredictably from multiple directions, spontaneously exploiting gaps in the enemy's defenses as they arise. As we see later on, maneuver warfare amplifies the physical damage of attacks by disorienting and demoralizing the enemy through a reliance on leverage instead of mass.

MICRO-COMPETITORS

The idea of shifting emphasis from straightforward waves of large attacks to multidirectional smaller ones is one to which many businesses should be able to relate. In a world where information and communications technologies allow the near-instantaneous dissemination of a vast number of new ideas, and where once-unified groups of people have fractured into tribes and micromarkets, the momentum has moved from established giant companies to nimble, fast-growing start-ups.

Few companies understand this shift better and fear it more than Microsoft. Though the company has plenty of critics, few can accuse it of letting itself be caught by surprise by any of the hundreds of firms, wielding any number of new technologies, that have popped up to threaten the company's domination in the volatile computer industry. For example, by early 1999 Microsoft had already established a team of engineers and marketers dedicated to doing nothing but keeping track of develop-

ments with Linux, the software operating system that has
gained favor among a tiny but rapidly growing percentage of
computer users.

The apparent drawback to maneuver warfare is the enormous dif-
ficulty involved in coordinating, or even tracking, the movements of
a relatively large number of smaller groups of soldiers who are constantly shifting their position and plans, usually over a wider area.
How can accurate, firsthand information about the battlefield—what
the Marines call "ground truth"—be passed up the chain, and orders
passed back down, quickly enough to control the battle? Maneuver
warfare values dynamicism over all else, and there are times when the
long, tall hierarchy clearly can't keep up.

"Because of how long it takes reports to filter up through the
chains," says Randy Gangle, "there can be three hours' difference
between the tactical picture seen by the front lines and the one seen by
the commanders. That time translates to distance. In three hours the
enemy can move from here all the way to there." Says another colonel:
"It's like playing telephone. Information goes from the fire team to the
squad to the platoon to the company to the battalion to the [force]
commanders to high headquarters. By that time it's not useful."

A NEW COMPLEXITY

At the same time that the Marines were changing their basic tactics, a
large shift was also taking place in the view of the type of battlefield
onto which the Marines were likely to be called into action. Marines
had long specialized in beach invasions and were also trained and
experienced in fighting on forest, jungle, and desert terrains. But by
the early 1990s it seemed clear that the Marines could expect a growing percentage of their missions to be based in urban settings.

For one thing, the world's population is increasingly huddling in
cities. In the 1940s one-quarter of Western Europe's population lived

in cities; now over three-quarters are urban dwellers. Worldwide about two billion people live in cities, and at current migration and population growth rates that number will increase to six billion by 2025. One study by the military indicated that of the twenty-seven ground-force engagements the United States has engaged in over the past two decades, only six were entirely nonurban. The other twenty-one all involved some urban warfare, and ten were fought entirely within the boundaries of one or more cities.

In the past perhaps half the cities in the world weren't close enough to the ocean to be considered within the Marines' ordinary mission. But current generations of helicopters and amphibious vehicles allow the Marines to mount full-scale attacks two hundred miles inland—a zone that covers approximately 80 percent of the world's population. In addition, the Marines' embassy and other evacuation missions normally bring them into cities, regardless of the proximity of the conflict sites to the sea.

Combat is a complex environment under the best of circumstances, but the urban environment adds a number of complications. The area may be densely packed with enormous populations of noncombatants on all sides; often these are the very people the Marines have been sent in to protect or rescue. It may be unacceptable to damage buildings or roads, even without the loss of innocent life. "We don't want to be in the position of rubbling cities and creating streams of refugees and instability," says Lieutenant Colonel John Allison. "We'd end up with more problems postconflict than we had preconflict."

But at the same time that Marines have to be extra cautious with their fire, notes Allison, they are also at extreme risk when patrolling the city, which can harbor snipers in any window and ambushes around any corner, as well as nonuniformed attackers who can't readily be distinguished from nonhostile civilians in street crowds. "Historically it's a high-casualty environment," he says. "You can lose an entire infantry battalion in a few blocks."

The Marines summarize the complexity of the urban warfare environment with the term "three-block war": within the span of three blocks a Marine may encounter friendly citizens, a mob of rioters, and heavily armed combatants. In Somalia the very people whose families were being fed by the Marines sometimes took up arms against them hours later. It's a problem analogous to one faced by some business managers every day: the line between customer, partner, and competitor is blurring, sometimes very quickly. A simple example: if you're selling goods over the Internet, should you set up a link to another site that is referring customers to your site but is also partnering with your competitors? The Marines describe these confusing, hard-to-pin-down, nontraditional threats as "asymmetric." Increasingly asymmetric threats are the ones that are demanding the most attention, in the Marine and the business world alike.

Adding to the problem is that the stakes of such decisions are typically far higher in urban warfare than they are in other battle environments. It's what one officer calls "the CNN factor": because on-the-scene television news crews quickly get word—and sometimes even footage—out on provocative events such as civilian casualties, it is no longer unlikely that a nineteen-year-old Marine's actions will reverberate in headlines around the world the next day. "These are tactical decisions with strategic implications," says Gangle. "We've seen it with the British in Ireland, where a Brit corporal takes fire, orders return fire, someone hits a woman walking down the street, and three hours later the prime minister is explaining to Parliament why the peace talks are breaking down."

Unfortunately, in highly uncertain, risky, and mixed-mission environments such as these, where decisions can carry such phenomenal weight, Marines are least likely to be able to access the chain of command. For one thing, there may not be enough time to make it up even one rung of the ladder when a Marine stumbles into a mob brandishing weapons. But even if the Marine does have a few moments to shout into his radio, there's a good chance the message won't get through, owing to the fact that radio communications are weakened or outright blocked by buildings. "It's a segmented, isolated battlefield," says Gangle. One colonel remembers that in Nairobi he wasn't able to supervise directly units that were a few blocks away from him. What's more, multiple urban conflicts may be taking place simultaneously in one large-scale mission, making it even harder for centralized command to function effectively and quickly, as was the case in Somalia.

Increasingly businesses face much the same sorts of problems. When Disney acquired the Internet portal provider Infoseek, even the big raises and stock benefits it passed out couldn't prevent an exodus of key talent from Infoseek. The reported reason: Disney insisted on foisting its environment—one in which top managers approve everything—on the Internet firm, and the marketplace was changing in less time than it took for potential responses to go up and down the Infoseek-Disney chain. Or consider Northwest Airlines, whose centralized control of airport decisions left local managers helpless to manage a pileup of stranded, passenger-filled planes during a blizzard in Detroit, earning the company one of the worst public relations disasters in recent memory.

AUTHORITY ON DEMAND

Maneuver warfare and the trend to urban fighting have made it increasingly dubious that the conventional chain of command can at all times control the actions of the Marines who are actually aiming the weapons. If the chain of command can't process information and hand down effective decisions quickly enough, there's only one solution: the lower links of the chain have to make their own decisions.

The answer, in other words, is empowerment, but not the corporate brand of empowerment we're used to hearing about. This isn't about allowing customer service reps to accept a damaged item on return, or a front-desk clerk to comp a hotel guest on breakfast. This is about allowing someone at the lowest level of the organization to make decisions that can affect the success of the organization's most important missions. What's more, Marine empowerment allows lower-level officers and enlisted to commandeer resources and jettison preestablished plans.

Clearly if all Marines operated continually in this mode there would be mass confusion, redundant and conflicting missions, and too many bad decisions. To avoid such chaos, the Marines have found a way to fit their brand of hyper-empowerment into the framework of their narrow hierarchy. When time, situational, and communication constraints allow, Marines coordinate with other units or get strategic direction by staying within the chain of command. But they readily step out of the chain to take advantage of a fast-breaking opportunity, deal with an unfolding crisis, or cope with a loss of command contact. That's the scheme I call "authority on demand."

PRINCIPLE #6: BUILD AUTHORITY ON DEMAND INTO THE HIERARCHY

With authority on demand built into the hierarchy, Marines can shed the hierarchy and use their own judgment when the action becomes fast and furious. Officers at all levels start making decisions that might normally come from a colonel. Even privates know they are expected to take whatever initiative is necessary to complete a mission. In this way, says Colonel Schmidle, the Corps can have its cake and eat it, too, when it comes to organizational structure. "Command is by nature centralized," he says, "but you can decentralize control under it. If the environment you're dealing with is complex, there will be times when the more you try to control it the less control you'll have. Having that element of decentralization makes us more adaptive, and that allows us to deal better with chaos."

The move to authority on demand simply extends a long-held belief of the Marines: the best soldiers are those who follow orders from above but aren't dependent on orders. Says General Steele: "One of the reasons [German General Erwin] Rommel became such an effective decision-maker was that he grew up with mountain combat, where there's little communication with commanders." Steele says the lightbulb went on for him three decades ago when he was a captain and had the idea of taking his seventy-five men on a five-day swamp march; they improvised rafts, lived on rice, and in general got some realistic preparation for the rigors that awaited them in their upcoming postings to Vietnam. But the swamp march wasn't part of the standard training program, so Steele went to his colonel to ask his permission. "He said to me, 'There's the Army way and the Marine way,'" recalls Steele. "'The Army way is, don't do it unless someone says you can. The Marine way is, do it unless someone says you can't.'" Steele took off for the swamps the next day.

The Marine practice of taking on authority when the opportunity presents itself is sometimes jarring to officers from the other military services. One Marine colonel relates the story of a visiting Air Force colonel who asked a Marine sergeant to make sure housing was arranged for a large group of Air Force personnel scheduled to visit a few weeks later. When the Air Force colonel asked the sergeant the next day whether he had followed up on the request, he was shocked when the sergeant assured him that he had already made most of the arrangements. The Air Force colonel had intended for the sergeant to relay the request to the appropriate officer, not to act on it himself. The Marine sergeant, for his part, couldn't imagine why the Air Force colonel seemed disturbed that he had given the colonel exactly the results he had asked for.

A general recalls that during the Gulf War a platoon found itself under fire from an Iraqi machine gunner. A corporal from East Los Angeles decided to take action. He divided his squad in half, sent one of the groups to dig in at a relatively safe distance in front of the gunner, and then took the other half skirting around the gunner's side, where they surprised him. "It was a drive-by shooting," the corporal later explained to his lieutenant.

POWER TO THE LOWER RANKS

Some companies have made at least modified versions of authority on demand an integral part of their environment. It's not surprising that Hire Quality is one of them. The Chicago-based firm, which places former military personnel in jobs in the private sector, is founded and run by a former Marine captain, Dan Caulfield. The firm is something of an oddity in that Caulfield has attempted to import not merely a loose adaptation of the Marine Corps environment but a close replica in some regards, going so far as to urge his sixty employees to read Marine manuals and refer to the different functions in the company by the technical Marine designations for intelligence, operations, and logistics. The employees, most of whom have no military experience, seem entirely enthusiastic about the concept, especially with regard to authority on demand.

One Hire Quality employee, Da-Nay Rockmore, works over the phone with job candidates, trying to determine which positions might best suit them. As in her last job with a placement firm, she sits in front of a computer that displays a checklist for categorizing skills and experience. But unlike her previous company, Hire Quality encourages her to throw the list aside and match the candidate to a job based on her instincts. "At my last job, candidates were automatically disqualified by their answers," she says. "Here, it's my decision if the match is a good one." She notes that she recently placed a candidate who had driven trucks for the Army in a computer-oriented job, having determined that he was a fast learner and comfortable with technology; he's doing well at the job. Encouraged by her success at Hire Quality, Rockmore is now thinking about going to college part-time to get a business degree.

(A cautionary note: Explicitly military practices and themes don't always go over so well. In 1999 the clothing retail giant Limited Inc. rolled out an internal management motivation campaign based on war, including film clips of artillery attacks and wounded soldiers. Managers were reportedly so offended that some promptly quit.)

Griffin Hospital also practices authority on demand. The head of patient-care services, Vice President Lynn Werdal, recalls the time a patient was due in one of the labs for an echocardiogram but didn't feel well enough to be moved. "The nurse in the lab just decided to wheel the machine down to his room and do it there, even though no one had ever done that before," she says. "She didn't feel she had to ask my permission or anyone else's, and I like that."

The results of encouraging employees to take initiative can far exceed management's expectations. At the Regent Square Tavern in Pittsburgh, a waitress took it on herself to learn sign language so that she could better communicate with a regular patron who was deaf. Word soon got around, and now the Tavern attracts deaf customers from all around the city.

SMALL TEAMS: THE LEVERAGE POINT

Of course, imbuing lower levels in the organization with the power of authority on demand would be disastrous if people at those levels didn't understand the missions being carried out or weren't capable of taking actions to help accomplish the mission. The reason authority works so well in the Marines, as we see in coming chapters, is that Marine officers learn how to give orders in a way that complements authority on demand, and Marines of even the lowest ranks are trained to apply that authority effectively.

In fact, while most organizations tend to lavish attention on managers in proportion to how high up the ladder they are, it's at the lowest level of Marine leadership—the corporal—that the Corps has focused the lion's share of its skills development efforts in recent years. The Corps believes that a corporal and his or her three-or-four-person fire team is the leverage point for the Corps' actions. It's in these small units, Marines believe, that battles are won or lost, especially in the fast-changing, chaotic environments of maneuver and urban warfare. And it's here that contact with the chain of command is most likely to be either lost or useless, because of the limits of communications technology and the speed at which these teams must make decisions and act.

Left to itself, all management tends to drift toward pulling authority up and away from the lower ranks—even in the Marines. Up through the Vietnam War, Marine sergeants were well trained in letting corporals exercise their own judgment. But over the next two decades sergeants became micromanagers. General Charles C. Krulak, the Thirty-First Marine Corps commandant, campaigned hard to reverse that trend and to restore authority to the corporal and the fire team.

PRINCIPLE #7: FOCUS ON THE SMALL TEAM

The mock battle in downtown Camp Lejeune illustrates how authority on demand works with small units in chaotic situations. There is nothing rote about the exercise; in fact, to the Marines' knowledge, the battle marks the first time an actual U.S. town (albeit one on a Marine base) has been used as the site of a large, realistic military exercise.

The town is meant to represent a Third World urban environment. (The Marines refrain, as a matter of diplomacy, from explicitly identifying in any official form the actual countries they're pretending to invade in exercises. The area, or "playbox," is given over to "free play" for the Marines who are impersonating enemy army troops, armed insurgents—the Landrones—and gang members. That is, these Marines are told to do anything they want to make life difficult for the Marine invasion force. To complicate matters, a number of Lejeune residents are playing the roles of innocent civilians scattered throughout the playbox, minding their own business.

The invasion force comes in from the beach at 3:00 A.M., facing first tank-supported resistance from the ersatz army, and then a riot. The Marines break these up and spread out through the town. Soon scuffles are breaking out all over as the army soldiers and Landrone militiamen manage to pull together small attacks and various gangs engage in hit-and-run tactics. The Marines start hunting the enemy down, with the goal of restoring peace and order to the town.

There is no lack of commanders. At a temporary headquarters office set up in a nearby building, ten officers, mostly captains, huddle around a table, hunched over hand-held radios. Stuck together in one room, the officers are not playing their roles realistically—in a real invasion, they would be scattered at positions as near as possible to the three platoons in each of their companies. But the exercise is meant to be realistic to the Marines under them, and from the point of view of these soldiers, the captains are involved only as disembodied voices on the radio, just as they would be for the most part in a real mission.

An untrained observer—and for that matter most trained observers—wouldn't have been able to make heads or tails of the various small battles that spring up and then evaporate throughout the final hours of the night. A tank comes rumbling across a field, swings its turret toward an invisible target, fires, and then rumbles off again. Humvees rush by in all directions. Sporadic gunfire can be heard first in one building and then, after a few minutes of silence, in another one.

The fighting carries into the early hours of sunlight, and then the exercise is halted so that the Marines can rehash what happened and figure out what went wrong and what went right. By the time the Marines are finally given a few hours off, it's almost noon, and the temperature hovers around 100 degrees, with 95 percent humidity. Some manage to find a small patch of shade and fall immediately asleep. Others break into their MREs—plastic bags of high-calorie food inside a metal pouch that contains a chemical heating element. On the menu today: squishy light brown stuff or squishy dark brown stuff.

I speak to Corporal Gary Hansen, who is sprawled out next to a tree but having trouble drifting off in the heat. A large man in his early twenties, he is clearly exhausted. Hansen explains that he's a team leader for a machine-gun squad, consisting of seven people riding in two Humvees adorned with fifty-caliber machine guns. Even though most of the men were equipped with night-vision goggles, it was nearly impossible, he notes, to tell where the firing was coming from as they prowled around the town. "You don't know if it's friendly or enemy," he says with a shrug.

At a few points Hansen's squad hooked up with other squads equipped with missiles and other heavier weapons, supporting them by drawing enemy fire. Other times the squad chased down sniper fire. Once the squad encountered an enemy unit that had taken over a local club. "We spun around the church, took cover, laid down suppressing fire, and then called in an airstrike," he recalls.

Though Hansen had a radio and received a fairly constant stream of orders from the platoon commander, almost none of the orders proved useful. "The orders would change five times before we got to execute it," he says. "We had to call it as it was happening. There was no time to call someone up and wait for decisions." Whatever brief time there was to use the radio, he adds, was generally spent speaking not with commanders but with fellow squad leaders of the platoon to coordinate attacks and provide each other with warnings.

I also speak with a staff sergeant, Rigo Guzzman, who is in charge of a squad of four tanks. Wearing round wire-rimmed glasses that somehow fail to soften his looks, Guzzman is sitting on top of the tank with other members of the squad picking at the remains of an MRE. Thanks to the tank skin's ability to soak up the sunlight, it's so hot that the MREs' chemical heating element doesn't need to be activated. Inside the tank it's even hotter. "Our air-conditioning filters clogged," Guzzman explains.

During the night Guzzman's tank was sent by commanders after a number of targets, but few of them turned out to be enemy strongholds or vehicles. Instead, the enemy tended to turn up without warning. "We were told to secure a building that had been cleared of the enemy, but as soon as we approached we started taking fire from it," recounts Guzzman. "We put two explosive rounds into the building, and that took care of it." Another time a heavily armed vehicle came zigzagging down the road toward them, and Guzzman couldn't get whoever was manning the vehicle on the radio. The tank took the vehicle out with machine-gun fire.

In both cases the decision to fire in a confusing, unexpected situation was made not by Guzzman but by the corporal manning the guns. "I give him a lot of leeway," Guzzman explains. "I tell him to just give me a quick holler, and then light them up." (The holler, if nothing else, gives Guzzman a chance to put his fingers in his ears against the hellish bark of the tank's main gun.) Other squads tell similar stories: though higher-ups were determining the mission the squad had to run, it was frequently corporals who made the critical call to fight or not fight and who selected targets.

(One thing that most businesses don't understand yet is that it's not just young Marines who are ready to take on more responsibility. According to a report based on a 1999 poll of eighteen- to thirty-year-olds conducted by Peter Hart Research Associates, "young people overwhelmingly describe a model of leadership that is built from the bottom up.")

FINDING THE RIGHT LEVEL OF DECENTRALIZATION

In addition to pushing a tremendous amount of authority down to the level of corporal, the Corps has also acted to decentralize tactical command to the company level. (A company, remember, typically consists of three platoons and contains between ninety and two hundred Marines.) But the decentralization is selective, focusing on the type of authority that has the most impact on the mission—that is, on faster, more effective responses to complex, changing environments. At the same time the Corps has taken away less critical types of authority from the company commander and lifted them up the ladder. "When I was a company commander in Vietnam," says General Steele, "I had my own mess [food service], administrative, and supply. Now those sorts of things are being centralized to free up the company commander and let the company serve as a tactical headquarters. That captain now doesn't have as many administrative decisions to make, and more tactical decision-making authority."

A more delicate issue is the extent to which battle information is centralized. On the one hand, providing detailed, raw information from the front lines to high-level commanders can help those commanders make better strategic decisions and offer more support to the company. On the other hand, having that sort of information can lead to micromanagement. "It's always tempting to reach down and pull more authority up, and we try to be careful about that," says Steele. "Sometimes when that happens it's not the commander who's doing it, it's someone on his staff. If that's the case, then the captain has a duty to speak to the commander to tell him that it's interfering with his operation."

In many organizations going over your boss's head is considered bad form, and potentially suicidal career-wise. In the Marines it's not only safe but encouraged, provided you've made a reasonable effort to work things out through your boss. If that effort has been made and has failed, then a Marine of any rank is welcome to contact superior officers anywhere in the chain of command, right up to the commandant. Marine policy is to never reprimand a Marine for taking his or her case to an officer of too high a rank; at worst, the Marine may be told to continue to work through the chain of command. At the same time informal policy also dictates not coming down hard on a Marine's direct commander when a complaint is made (assuming it doesn't involve serious charges). Marines are encouraged to jump up through the chain not as a way to get superior officers in trouble but to find better ways of doing things.

THANK YOU FOR GOING OVER MY HEAD

H. Lee Scott, chief operating officer of Wal-Mart, has told of being called into the office of the company founder, Sam

Walton, early in Scott's career after a number of truck drivers complained about the imperious way he was supervising them. After Walton discussed the problem with him, Walton ushered in each of the complainants so that Scott could personally thank them for bringing the problem to senior management's attention.

FINDING THE RIGHT SIZE AND MIX

It's not simply in terms of the fluidity of its hierarchy and the distribution of authority that the Marine structure is distinguished from that of other organizations. An equally defining difference is the Corps' on-the-fly malleability in the size and mix of its functional units.

Like any military service, the Marines are broken down for administrative purposes into divisions, regiments, and battalions—a structure roughly analogous to business units, product lines, and departments of a corporation. But these traditional, well-defined compartmentalizations have little to do with the way the Marines function. Instead, the Marines think in terms of more fluid, customizable groupings.

At the heart of these groupings is the concept of the Marine Air-Ground Task Force, or MAGTF (pronounced "mag-taf"), a unit of no set size or composition that draws together various Marine groups into a tightly integrated force capable of carrying out a major operation, be it an invasion, a police action, an evacuation, or a relief mission.

The best-known, best-defined incarnation of a MAGTF is a three-ship MEU. Though a MEU in many ways epitomizes the Marine Corps' capabilities, a MAGTF doesn't have to be a MEU, or even resemble a MEU. A MAGTF can be anything from a full-scale invasion force of tens of thousands of Marines supported by hundreds of aircraft to a couple of platoons backed up by a helicopter. What's more, a MAGTF can be, and frequently is, "globally sourced"—that is, assembled piecemeal from different Marine battalions around the world. MAGTFs can look like the classic infantry and air-support units well suited to storming a beach and taking a town, or they can be ad hoc, one-of-a-kind combinations of Marine specialties, vehicles, and weapons designed to carry out an unusual function, like the special-purpose MAGTF sent into Los Angeles to help quell the riots.

MAGTFs have their own command elements—that is, there is always a MAGTF commander and staff. But because a MAGTF is frequently assembled, at least in part, of conventional units like battalions and companies, there are also usually independent and parallel chains of command within the MAGTF. Though all commanders within the MAGTF are subordinate to the MAGTF commander, they are often given leeway to function largely as they see fit, with the MAGTF commander serving primarily to help track and coordinate the decisions and actions of the various commanders under him or her. The different groups, or "cells," that make up a MAGTF may be preexisting units, or they may be units patched together specifically for the MAGTF's needs.

Why would the Marines employ such an improvisational, loose, and apparently confusing arrangement as their primary structure for accomplishing missions? Marines believe that no matter how intelligently an organization is carved into fixed functional units, none of those units will exactly meet the needs of a particular mission, with all its special conditions and complexities. Instead, say the Marines, each mission needs its own unique MAGTF, with a customized size and combination of capabilities. The Marines call this practice "task-organizing."

PRINCIPLE #8: TASK-ORGANIZE

The Marines have achieved a great deal of expertise in quickly bringing together the right mix of skills and equipment to custom-build a MAGTF for a particular mission. These mixes cross the boundaries not only of conventional units, like regiments, but also of different functions within the units.

Conventional military forces, like most corporations, have clearly defined functions within a clearly defined unit. Thus, a business has a subsidiary that manufactures a particular line of products, and that subsidiary has a marketing department, an accounting department, a personnel department, and so forth. Analogously, a traditional military unit has an intelligence group, an operational group, a logistics group, and other subunits.

The Marines need all the traditional functions, of course. They just don't organize them in traditional ways. The Marines have units dedicated to particular functions, such as air wings, but this arrangement is primarily for administrative and training purposes. Such dedicated units serve as pools of skills from which any MAGTF can draw as it's being pulled together. In this way, the Marines strike a balance between the efficiency of preparing standardized units and the flexibility of building units from scratch for each mission.

The MAGTF may be far larger or far smaller than the individual pools from which it draws. For example, a Marine regiment may include infantry, logistics, and air support groups. A MAGTF can draw on pieces of each of these groups to form a miniature version of the regiment. Or it can combine groups from several regiments to form a division-size unit with the same mix of functions. The MAGTF can have a fractal structure: though the scale may change drastically, the basic mix remains the same.

In theory, a MAGTF can also create extremely lopsided mixes of specialties. For example, the Marines may want to create a MAGTF with significant air support to carry out a campaign that's heavy on bombing and lighter on ground troops. Such lopsided missions, however, are typically undertaken by the Army, Navy, and Air Force, which, after all, are by definition lopsided in their capabilities. The Marines prefer missions that call for integrated capabilities. Marine leaders can sound surprisingly New-Age discussing their "holistic" and "organic" styles of operation.

THE CORPORATE MAGTF

VeriFone is one business that has incorporated a MAGTF-like flexibility into its working structure. Instead of maintaining rigid, traditional departments, teams spring into existence on an as-needed basis, drawing however many people they need, and from whatever specialties are required (usually a combination of marketing, engineering, and support personnel), to accomplish the task at hand. What's more, many of the people pulled into a team participate via travel or videoconference because they are typically not from the office where the team leader is based but from offices around the world. For years a number of VeriFone clients around the United States and the world thought that the company was headquartered near their own location because so many VeriFone employees from so many different departments seemed to be at their disposal when a need arose. In fact less than 7 percent of VeriFone's 2,800 employees work in Silicon Valley at the official headquarters—which is called the official headquarters only because the SEC insisted that some office be so designated in the company's filings.

LOGISTICS

If the Marines had to point to one functional area within the MAGTF where they have achieved something approaching mastery in integration, it would be logistics—providing all the supplies and services needed to sustain a fast-moving Marine operation for weeks at a time. "Every commander knows that logistics is the Achilles' heel of every operation," says one general. Or as Eisenhower is said to have put it: "Anyone can draw a big blue arrow on the map. The hard part is supplying it."

Providing logistics support for a Marine operation can be a mind-boggling affair. Large operations require that virtually an entire working city be constructed in days, including the equivalent of supermarkets, post offices, water and power utilities, and much more. Smaller operations require supplying fast- and unpredictably moving combat units must be supplied with a steady supply of "beans, bullets, and Band-Aids," as the Marines put it. (The supply item most frequently requested by infantry platoons outside of food and ammunition, and the most costly: batteries.)

There are a phenomenal number of details to keep track of. Logistics commanders, for example, station people at major ports around the world to ensure that Marine equipment shipments coming through don't get hung up on the docks. Oddly enough, Marines are a great deal easier to ship around than the things they need. When a large MAGTF has to be formed and brought across the world in a hurry, the Marines are sometimes shipped out in a matter of hours in large Air Force planes; when they reach their destination, they're met by merchant ships that have been prestocked with needed equipment and supplies and are kept floating around throughout the world. It's a feat of planning, coordination, and transportation, and it all has to be capable of changing on the fly.

WINNING THROUGH LOGISTICS

Companies like Wal-Mart and Federal Express have virtually defined themselves through logistics excellence. Now the CEOs of many high-flying Internet companies are just discovering how hard logistics is, and how important: it's one thing to capture a big market share with attractive prices and a convenient shopping experience, but it's another to make money on the whole thing by being able to deliver the product at a low-enough cost to leave a profit margin. Consider, for example, how difficult it will be for most online grocery vendors to compete against the Webvan Group, which placed an order for $1 billion worth of automated warehousing facilities in 1999. One

Internet-based merchant, Commercekey, even has a MEU-like fleet of cargo vessels standing by to deliver goods around the world.

Among the pools of functional expertise maintained by the Marines, the logistics pools are often the largest. Outside of missions, logistics groups typically operate as full battalions with massive arrays of equipment and vehicles. Almost every unit of any significant size in the Marines has what the Marines call an "organic" logistics function—a relatively small group capable of serving the basic needs of the unit. MEUs, for example, include 270 Marines dedicated to logistics. But when a MAGTF is formed, the organic group is usually supplemented with a chunk of support from a logistics battalion. A typical combat division, for example, maintains about half a dozen five-ton trucks; a logistics division maintains about six hundred. All Marines must be prepared to transfer their fierce battalion loyalty to the MAGTF, but it's particularly true of Marines attached to logistics battalions. "We never see one of our battalions go anywhere as a battalion," says Colonel J. B. Beavers, who commands a logistics group at Camp Lejeune. Just one of the consequences of this structure is that logistics divisions must deal with a constant influx and outflow of talent.

The most intelligently designed organizational structure in the world won't do much good if the organization can't develop the managerial talent it needs to fill the upper layers of that structure. The next two chapters examine how the Corps pulls off the difficult task of finding, educating, and polishing great managers, a job that many businesses find to be their biggest challenge.

$$\star \quad \star \quad \star \quad \star \quad \star$$

4. EDUCATING MANAGERS

Robert E. Lee (no relation) was a Marine second lieutenant in 1975 when he was shipped over to Vietnam during the evacuation at the end of the war, one month before the fall of Saigon. His first order: take a dozen Marines, board one of the merchant ships packed with refugees, and secure it from the bands of deserting South Vietnamese soldiers who were seizing ships and killing the crews. No word on how he was supposed to go about boarding and securing a ship, something the Marines hadn't made part of their repertoire for about a hundred years. Just do it.

After necessarily brief reflection, Lee hit on the following insight: the ship had several decks, so why not treat it like a big building with many floors? Securing a building was something he had been taught to do. You start at the top, so that gravity works in your favor (you can drop down on opponents faster than they can climb up to you, and you don't have to worry about hand grenades bouncing back down). Deck by deck, he and his men secured the ship.

Lee, now a trim, blue-eyed colonel, might be considered the Marines' top trainer. He tells this "sea story," among many others, to the hundreds of newly minted, barely twenty-something second lieutenants who come under his care and tutelage each year. Sea stories are not merely an important means for transferring wisdom from experienced Marine officers to younger ones; they are the primary means. This particular sea story is especially useful, not because it teaches young officers how to command a boarding party—something they are highly unlikely to do at any point in their careers—but rather because it speaks directly to two of the Marines' most closely held beliefs. Namely:

1.   War is confusion and the unexpected. As a Marine officer, you either learn to embrace it, and even turn it to your advantage, or you find another career.

2.   Because of this difficult fact, the only way to succeed is to have at your disposal a wide set of knowledge "templates," at least one of which can, with a little creativity, be applied to the situation at hand.

Entrusting mid- and low-rank officers with critical battle decisions forces the Marines to pay close attention to the skills of the people they invest with these responsibilities. Installing effective decisionmakers at lower levels is an essential and obvious requisite to pushing down authority in any organization, but even companies that consider themselves committed to decentralization rarely make the hiring and training of managers as high a priority as do the Marines. One element of this process that especially distinguishes the Corps from most organizations is the tremendous emphasis it has placed on in-house management education.

THE MANAGEMENT-TALENT FILTER

Driving down the long Quantico base road, you first pass through a country club–like sprawl of lush, rolling hills. But these gradually give way to flatter, harsher-looking terrain composed of a thousand shades of drab, until you finally find yourself surrounded by buildings that look like barracks. But Quantico never quite descends to the scoured-out look of a military base; rather, it resembles an unusually uncharming college campus, which in some ways it is.

Only ten percent of Marine officers hail from the Naval Academy. (The Marines have no college academy of their own, but Annapolis graduates have the option of entering the Corps.) For all other Marine officers, the first postrecruitment experience with the Corps is at the Marine base at Quantico, Virginia, home to the unique ordeal of Officer Candidate School. "School" is something of a misnomer: the primary purpose of Marine OCS is not to teach but rather to screen out those who might be lacking in the right stuff; it is essentially a ten-week, seven-day-a-week, twenty-four-hour-a-day job interview. The OCS commander, Colonel John Lehockey, is the first to admit that this is a ridiculous amount of time to spend evaluating a prospective manager. "It's not nearly long enough," he sighs. Though the already carefully screened candidates are put through a grueling treadmill of physical and academic challenges at OCS, they are most carefully scrutinized, according to Lehockey, for their leadership qualities. "It has no exact definition," he notes. "It's our job to recognize it."

As with boot camp recruits, OCS candidates have in effect been conditionally hired. And like boot camp, OCS provides candidates (at least those who aren't already Marines) with a jolting transition from civilian life. Colonel Rick Zilmer remembers when his friendly regional Marine recruiter stepped onto the bus he had boarded for Quantico with other officer candidates from his area. Bidding the group farewell, the recruiter said, "Gentlemen, it's hard to visualize hell. . . ."

Though the verbal, mental, and physical abuse of OCS doesn't quite measure up to that of boot camp, it is nonetheless formidable. Recruits are herded at a run from ten-mile marches to grueling calisthenics to crawls through mud. In between, they get doses of classroom and field training, with never quite enough food and sleep to reenergize them. Like boot camp recruits, they have to run the infamous "Crucible" obstacle course.

There are important differences, though, between OCS and boot camp. A Marine who makes it through boot camp is considered ready to perform the basic functions expected of a Marine in combat—in particular, he or she is proficient at riflery. An OCS graduate hasn't had nearly enough training in hands-on infantry skills to qualify as a combat-ready Marine. "An OCS graduate isn't up the standards of a Marine private," says Lehockey.

What's more, boot camp recruits are deemed fit to be Marines for the most part according to their ability to not break down under the stress; those who hang in there are generally welcomed to the Corps. In OCS, candidates don't have to start crumbling before they're screened out, or even walk out. Any candidate can leave at any time simply by saying the word, no questions asked. But more important, candidates can also fail to graduate by displaying a dearth of physical, intellectual, or leadership skills. In this sense, OCS could be seen as less like a boot camp and more like a conditional hiring: new hires are thrown into a demanding, sink-or-swim environment designed to separate out the poor fits.

PRINCIPLE #9: HIRE THROUGH TRIAL BY FIRE

Of the abilities tested at OCS, leadership is most likely to be the stumbling block; it accounts for 50 percent of each candidate's grade. From five o'clock in the morning when candidates are rousted from bed until ten o'clock that night when the lights are turned out, candidates are scrutinized for any sign that they are endowed with more or less than their share of ability to motivate and direct their fellow candidates.

There is no situation from which clues to leadership ability can't be derived, insists Lehockey. "We have a saying," he explains. "'Wherever there are two Marines, one of them is a leader.' Most everyone here believes the way to make it through is to blend in. But to be an outstanding performer here you've got to step out." Shortly after arriving at OCS, the 200 or so new candidates are told to grab a box lunch off a waiting truck, and to make it snappy. "They think they're taking a break," says Lehockey, "but we're watching to see if anyone tries to organize a line to speed things up. We're *always* watching." The candidates get a few days off during OCS, but even this break is a test of sorts: Lehockey and his crew want to see whether the candidates who are struggling with the academic material use the time to try to catch up rather than heading off to town for beers. As with all aspects of the Corps, perseverance counts for something at OCS.

One element of OCS is specifically designed to bring leadership abilities, or a lack thereof, to the fore. The "leadership reaction course," or LRC, is a series of what might very loosely be called brain-teasers. The problems are intensely hands-on though, and significantly, candidates are subjected to the scenarios in groups of four.

The course is a series of twenty adjoining cinder-block and wood cells open at the top, each containing large, heavy items ranging from wood platforms to metal tubes to chains. A mucky stream runs through ten of the cells. All in all, the course looks like a cross between a POW camp and the playground from hell.

Each cell represents a "problem" that the four candidates are supposed to "solve." Each roughly simulates a battlefield predicament. In one cell, for example, the candidates are told that they have to get a wounded comrade across the stream—a "deep-water gorge"—using a rope and boards. In another, they're required to get all four of themselves over a tall wall that seems to be unscalable. In yet another, they have to crawl along planks in a "sewer" tunnel. Some of the climbing surfaces are painted with patches of red, which are to be considered "mined" or otherwise deadly to the touch. Any candidate who touches red is pronounced dead and has to stand uselessly by the side for a minute or two until resurrected by an instructor. The ropes, sticks, chains, barrels, and other implements scattered through the cells may or may not be useful to solving the problem. "Sometimes we put in extra equipment," says Lehockey. "The engineers in the group think, if it's here, I'm supposed to use it."

Some of the problems are solvable, some aren't. But solving the problem isn't the point—whether they solve it or not doesn't even enter into the candidates' grades. Instead, the candidates are watched for how they handle themselves. "Which ones step up to take the lead?" says Lehockey. "Who asks for input from the others? Who recognizes when a plan is failing and backs off to try another?"

Candidates run the LRC twice during OCS. When they tackle it the first time, during the third week, none of the four candidates in a group is formally placed in charge. The four are briefed together on the problem by an instructor, and any of them can ask questions. Though the event isn't officially graded, the candidates are carefully observed.

When the candidates run the LRC again, near the end of OCS, one of the four candidates is appointed the leader for a problem and taken aside by the instructor for a private briefing. This time the leader is graded, and all the candidates get a chance to be the leader. "If you've been a jerk to everyone else for the past nine weeks, this is where it comes back to get you," says Lehockey.

The day I observe a group of candidates running the second, graded version of the LRC, it is raining, and all the equipment and climbing surfaces are slick with water. The candidates are soaked and exhausted, and any parts of their faces and arms not covered in camouflage grease paint are smeared with mud; it's even hard to distinguish the male from the female candidates. (The groups are segregated by sex.) Adding to the fun, the candidates have to speed-march three miles in between tackling each problem.

I watch with Lehockey as the leader of one group is led to the edge of a cell for his briefing, while the other three candidates are told to remain some thirty feet away. The leader listens, nods, asks a few questions, then dashes back to his group to fill them in. To me, the candidate has shown good enthusiasm, but Lehockey grunts and shakes his head. He explains to me that the leader shouldn't have run away from the problem to join his group; he should have signaled for the group to move forward to join him at the cell. The criticism may seem picky, but it points to an important leadership quality: a critical role of a leader is to get his or her people to step up to the challenge, in some cases literally.

The recipient of a different briefing also earns a grimace from Lehockey. "He's already starting to think about what he's going to do," he explains. "He's only half-listening, and he's missing details." These are mistakes that all candidates will learn to correct in the coming months. But Lehockey and his crew of instructors prefer candidates who do it the right way instinctively.

In one cell two candidates are struggling to pass a heavy ammunitions box across a "blown-up bridge" to the other two candidates. The leader places himself in a precarious spot in what seems to me a valiant effort to make the hand-off, but ends up brushing up against red paint. "Boom!" shouts the instructor; the leader is "dead." Does he get an A for effort? I ask Lehockey. No way. "If a leader takes himself out, it probably means he was endangering himself unnecessarily, probably by being too aggressive," he says. "Some leaders fail because they try to do it all themselves." Or as another officer puts it to me later, "Your people are looking to you for guidance," he says. "If you're too busy aiming, you'll let them down."

In another cell a group is trying desperately to lever a barrel over a large wood pyramid with poles. One candidate slips and drops his pole, which hits a red zone. "Boom!" yells the instructor. The leader looks stricken, and for several moments the group stands there, miserable. It's this loss of momentum, of course, rather than the dropped pole, that counts against the leader.

Next door the candidates are trying to help each other scratch their way to the top of a small wood tower checkerboarded with the dreaded red paint. One candidate tries leaping from the shoulders of another to purchase a hold on a wooden ledge near the top, but he slips backward and crashes his ribs against a beam. Lehockey hollers, "Corpsman!"—the Marine equivalent of "Medic!" and an unsettling thing to hear. The injured candidate is quickly tended to; he seems to have merely had the wind knocked out of him.

Throughout all the activity, instructors with clipboards watch dispassionately from catwalks up above. Each candidate who takes a turn as leader is rated by the instructors—mostly sergeants—as well as by the various officers on the school staff. (The leaders get no on-the-spot feedback because it might give unfair advantage to those who go later, but all the candidates get a detailed critique of their performance later.) Another important part of the evaluation is the rating candidates give to each other at four different points during OCS. Even the Crucible is a graded event, unlike the one in boot camp. "You have to be so focused to make it through OCS that it's like a laser burning a hole through you," says Lehockey. "Some candidates just run out of time."

In fact Marine OCS is regarded as such a concentrated, rigorous trial of character and ability that despite the prestige attached in all the services to having come up through the service's academy rather than its OCS, Marine officers who come in through the Naval Academy rather than OCS often express regret at having missed the chance to prove themselves under OCS conditions. (Not that anyone would claim the Naval Academy is a cakewalk.)

In the end, all the candidate evaluations are filtered through Lehockey, who makes the final decision about who passes and who doesn't. An average of about 25 percent of the candidates are washed out. Lehockey says a good fraction of those who are washed out probably would have made good Marine officers, but he has to err on the side of caution to keep out potential failures. Once the Marines say you're in, whether through OCS or boot camp, they're not going to give up on you easily. And apparently Lehockey isn't making too many mistaken judgments: only about 1 percent of the candidates who pass OCS end up leaving the Corps within a year. "If a business said it had a 1 percent defect rate, I'd say they were wasting resources being too efficient and could probably ease up," he says. "But as much as I care about these guys and want them to succeed, what I'm most concerned about are the forty marines they'll be rewarded with serving if they make it."

Lehockey clearly has no intention of easing up, but neither is he interested in having OCS leave any scars on future Marine officers. "We could grind them into dust in these exercises," he says. "But we're not trying make them feel broken and dispirited. We're trying to promote confidence and intuition. This experience gives them insight into themselves, and they'll apply these lessons in other situations, even if they never realize it." Even those who wash out are meant to get something out of the OCS experience, adds Lehockey. For one thing, they're free to try again later. In fact—feelings about perseverance being what they are in the Corps—having been previously washed out is held in a candidate's favor the next time around.

PUTTING CANDIDATES ON THE SPOT

A number of leading-edge businesses are adopting conditional hiring and trial-by-fire philosophies, if in significantly milder forms than the Marine version. At Amazon, for example, job candidates have to field offbeat riddles such as, "How would you design a car for a deaf person?" (Best answer: stick in earplugs and drive around.) Microsoft is famous for putting its candidates on the spot with a long series of brainteasers, such as, "Why are manhole covers round?" (One of several acceptable answers: a square cover could slip through the hole if positioned diagonally.) At the management consultancy firm Monitor Company, candidates have been made to go through mock meetings with "clients." One Monitor interviewee, an MBA graduate, has said that, when told by her interviewer that she had performed miserably, she asked for advice on how to do better for the sake of future interviews—a response that won her the job.

The highly regarded company Trilogy Software in Austin, Texas, manages to come close to some of the literal parameters of OCS. The company runs its new hires through a three-month program of classes from eight in the morning until midnight, seven days a week, on computer programming, product planning, and marketing. At the end of the ordeal they have to break into teams and put together rigorously evaluated presentations based on the sort of assignment they might be given in

the company. As with OCS, some candidates don't make it into
the ranks of full-fledged employees.

THE MBA OF LEADERSHIP

The candidates who make it through OCS become second lieutenants, and the property of Colonel Lee. Lee is, improbably, a
Brooklyn boy, with a résumé that seems to comprise the military
careers of ten busy men. He is keenly aware that of the dozen or so
schools a Marine officer might attend in a full career, he has been
given command of what most Marine officers would agree is by far
the Corps' most important: The Basic School, or TBS, a six-month
course that turns raw second lieutenants into functioning Marine
officers. "There is no school like this in the other services," he says.
"Or anywhere in the world."

TBS is not a nightmare of endurance and evaluation along the
lines of OCS. This is made clear to the successful, if exhausted, OCS
candidates at the completion of the Crucible, when they are met by
massive Marine helicopters—no more buses for them—that airlift
them across the Quantico base to the more expansive and slightly
more bucolic TBS grounds. There, current TBS students welcome
them with backslaps and assurances about the relatively calm
months to come. TBS isn't intended to wash anyone out or push
people to the breaking point. It's a bit like a physically rigorous and
generally more demanding version of an MBA program that happens
to teach military skills.

Some businesses have created in-house management training programs; McDonald's, for instance, operates its "Hamburger University"
north of Chicago. What sets TBS apart, however, is that it
unabashedly eschews imparting specific skills in favor of breeding
generic, high-speed, chaos-proof leadership. "Experts and specialists
are a dime a dozen," says Lee, dismissing in one fell swoop a century
of business management theory. "What the world needs is someone

who can absorb an entire organization, understand people, and motivate them."

The Marines don't trust any other organization to train leaders who are up to their standards. "We build leadership from the bottom up," says one captain. "The disadvantage to that is we don't get to bring brilliant people in from the outside. But it's also our greatest strength."

For one thing, TBS builds up its students' appreciation for the Marine values, a process that was begun in OCS. Though they are now officers, they receive far more orders than they get to give. That's partly because all officers, no matter how high their rank, have to take orders. But more important, the Marines believe that a manager won't appreciate the power of being able to demand obedience if he or she isn't experienced in offering obedience.

TBS students, though not regularly pressed to the edge of physical and mental exhaustion as they were in OCS, are still occasionally made to face daunting challenges both in the classroom and in the field. Care is taken, however, to ensure that they overcome them. The process builds confidence and allows them to become comfortable with the notion that with perseverance the seemingly impossible can be accomplished. In addition, training under extreme conditions will make the conditions of real missions much less likely to seem overwhelming.

PRINCIPLE #10: EMPLOY EXTREME TRAINING

As much as the Marines stress integrity throughout the Corps, rarely is it punched home with as much emphasis as at TBS. The message apparently gets through: only about one out of a thousand TBS students is discharged for "unacceptable behavior." (A handful of others will leave because they simply can't handle the workload.)

TBS also drives home the critical Marine belief in the necessity of individual styles of management and of bold, innovative decisions. "Contrary to the popular image, the Corps doesn't try to mold a single Marine personality," says Lee. "We harbor and protect eccentric characters. We want people who will invent the new mousetrap in battle. We teach lieutenants that they can't accept the status quo." When General Krulak came to address the students, he told them a story. The Roman council sent its army into Germana to wipe out rebellions there, overwhelming the poorly armed tribal warriors with archers, cavalry, and a large infantry. Three years later the council decided Germana needed a second thrashing and sent its legions back. But the tribes had a new strategy. They drew the archers into the woods to block their arrows, the cavalry into swamps to immobilize the horses, and the infantry into bogs. The message: the challenges you face tomorrow will not be the same ones you face today, so don't get stuck on a particular set of strategies and tactics.

Supporting this notion at TBS is a particularly liberal policy with regard to tolerating errors. "You don't get people to be innovative by beating them over the head if they do something that doesn't work out," says Lee. It's not surprising that even for a Marine Lee tends to be highly mistake-tolerant: his grades plummeted his final year at the Naval Academy in 1972 and he was about to be thrown out when a young captain by the name of Charles Krulak convinced the academy directors to let Lee be the first senior in the history of the academy to repeat the year.

Needless to say, TBS also inculcates in its students the Marine values of commitment to the Corps and interdependence. They're exposed to Corps traditions and to a myriad of both verbal assurances and hands-on demonstrations that challenges can be successfully met only through teamwork. Eventually TBS students come to see TBS itself—the only officer-level school in the entire military that is attended by every single officer in the service—as a large part of the bond they have with the Corps. "The way you get a shared vision is through a shared experience," says Lee. "The Basic School is the only common denominator to all Marine officers. We have reunions here twice a month that the current students attend, and when twenty-two-year-olds get to talk with seventy-year-olds about the same hikes, they make the connection."

TBS students take turns being commanders of platoons of their peers which provides two benefits: hands-on leadership experience for the students and the opportunity for instructors to observe a vast array of leadership styles. Students are given groundings in all the basic elements of Marine capabilities, from amphibious warfare to aviation to logistics. They also learn to respect enlisted officers' ability to get the job done and to rely on that ability. One small brain-teaser put to new students: "You, a sergeant, and two privates are given a certain amount of rope and some tools to erect a flagpole. How do you proceed?" The answer: "You say, 'Put up the flagpole, sergeant,' and leave." Because enlisted officers do much of the weapons and field exercise teaching at TBS, both the sergeants and the student lieutenants gain new respect for one another. (One sergeant instructor wrote an open letter to other enlisted officers after his TBS experience in which he took pains to note that TBS candidates "are in no way pampered or treated as if they are the missing link in the Marine Corps. Actually, it's quite the opposite. The rain, snow, or heat does not change the training schedule. It is a common occurrence to see a platoon of lieutenants, male and female, assaulting an objective soaking wet, tired, and miserable, but driving on and completing their mission, quite the same as we do [in enlisted officers' training].")

The atmosphere in TBS classes is friendly, lively, and hard-driving. Students salute Lee but seem casual around him; Lee never fails to return a salute without modifying it with a "How're ya doin'?" or the like. It's easy to overlook the fact that Lee holds a chunk of these officers' careers in his hands. Unlike their performance at OCS, which is strictly a pass-fail program, the students' performance at TBS becomes a permanent part of their record and can have a great deal of bearing on whether they end up on a fast track to the most desired jobs.

Though the students don't always know it, almost everything that happens to them at TBS carries a message. I observe a class on "nine-lines": developed by the Marines during the Korean War, this is the arcane but highly efficient way in which ground troops call in airstrikes. The class takes place in a large, community hall–like room whose walls are festooned with poster-sized maxims: "Tempo is itself a weapon"; "Each encounter in war will usually tend to grow increasingly disordered over time"; and so forth.

The six 45-person platoons of students have been divided in half to make for smaller teaching groups, and the captain-instructors have been shuffled around so that no student is being taught by either of the two captains normally assigned to his or her platoon, providing a little variety to cut down on tune-out and to broaden exposure to different leadership styles. Each group is huddled around four-by-eight-foot sandboxes mounted on tables. The sand in them is not the fine, clean sandbox variety; it looks more like dirt from a nearby ditch, which it probably is. Not that the Marines can't afford nicer sand. But they do prefer to do things in a grittier, more spartan way. Besides, the students might as well get used to it; they won't get high-quality sand shipped out to them when they're commanders in the field.

The sand on each of the sand-tables has been shaped into a number of mounds representing hills; each hill has a cardboard tag with a handwritten name: Amber, Georgia, Missouri, and others. These are code names, not the names of real hills. Like most information that Marines have to exchange during real-life missions, names and other details are obscured by jargon and simple codes to impair the chances, if only slightly, that an intercepted message will do the enemy any good. At any point in a conflict information is among the Marines' most precious resources, and they treat it with tremendous respect.

The recruits crowd close to the edge of the tables and lean over, revealing necks and skulls—the latter protected by about half a millimeter of hair—so sunburned that they're painful to look at. At the head of one table is a Captain Egerton, who is wearing camouflage paint on his face, apparently only because he feels like it. Egerton, a pilot outside of TBS, sports both a watch and a compass on his wrist.

With one hand, he's waving a long stick with a toy figurine of the Tazmanian Devil cartoon character glued to the end of it—the figurine represents the jet delivering the bombs—and with his other hand he's wielding a laser pointer whose lurid red dot designates various targets in the sand.

Nine-lines are so named because they comprise nine pieces of information that together present a simple and succinct way of indicating to a dispatcher the location of a target, what the plane should hit the target with, how it should approach the target, how it should recognize the target, and how it should exit the scene—all while minimizing the risk of hitting anything friendly or of getting hit itself by antiaircraft fire. This may sound straightforward enough in principle, but on first exposure it is a thoroughly baffling procedure conducted in a foreign language. Though Egerton is waving the Tazmanian Devil with great flair, there are several pairs of glazed eyes in the group.

It's unlikely that more than a few of these students will ever actually have to call in an airstrike in combat. Why teach it to them? Says Lee: "Even if you're in a motor pool, the lives of your fellow Marines may depend on your understanding how this works. You need to understand how the fog of war can affect situations, how they never happen the way you expect them to."

Egerton eases off some of the jargon and goes for simpler concepts. He gives his students a phrase they will hear hundreds of times in the coming years: "Big sky, little bullets," which refers to the fact that pilots tend not to worry too much about being hit by stray artillery shells. More broadly the slogan conveys the idea that before trying hard to avoid a potential problem, it's worth considering whether the chances of the problem occurring are extremely remote. In a complex, fast-changing environment, there are so many things to deal with that winning can come down to choosing the right things to ignore. Egerton also explains that it is up to the pilot to decide how much direction he wants to take from the person calling in the fire—even when you work collaboratively, it's important to establish ahead of time who has the final say when the question isn't settled by rank. And always be clear and concise, exhorts Egerton, repeating the phrase twice. "Macho infantry-speak doesn't cut it when you're dealing with a precise operation like a bombing run," he says. The penalty for screwing up? "The bombs can go short and land on you," he notes.

Egerton calls on one of the students to try his first nine-line. Everyone else looks relieved. The student forgets almost every step of the procedure. He performs every calculation incorrectly. He forgets that a "cardinal" is one of the four cardinal points of the compass. He gives a distance in "clicks"—macho infantry-speak for kilometers. Egerton doesn't give the hapless student any grief or show any impatience, but neither does he let up. When the student blanks out on the next step, Egerton puts a friendly hand on his shoulder. "Come on," he says. "What's your answer? Give it your best shot." After several long minutes Egerton helps the student wrestle the correct nine-line to the ground and tells him he did a terrific job. Now some of the other students seem eager to try.

TEACHING WITH SEA STORIES

The best-known bar in the Marine Corps is the Hawkins Room, alias The Basic School officers' club, a dark-wood-paneled affair set next to a Japanese tea garden. On the walls are an M-16 rifle (serial number 1), the sword of the legendary Marine commandant John Lejeune, a hatchet deeply embedded in a door frame, and a pewter mug reserved for the student company commander of the week. In a pointed reminder of the small privileges and large burdens of leadership, the student so honored gets to drink free beer all week long but almost never has time to take advantage of it.

Lee owns that he's never there less than four evenings a week. He doesn't have a drinking problem; he just knows that a significant percentage of the teaching about leadership takes place in the form of sea stories shared at the Hawkins Room. The staff knows they're expected to be there three times a week.

How do you teach leadership? The instructors at TBS can give classes on nine-lines, on equipping an infantry platoon, on using a map and compass, but they don't give classes on how to deal with disciplinary problems, how to lead people into battle, or how to take a ship from renegades.

There are no rules, no lists, no set processes that apply to any but the most rote of leadership situations, says Lee. Instead, TBS tries to hone decisionmaking the way a chessmaster does: through exposure to as many scenarios as possible so that the brain learns to recognize patterns it can apply as analogies to entirely new situations. That's how Lee solved his ship-securing problem, and that, he claims, is how all good managers solve the toughest challenges. Sea stories are the very best way to get these scenarios across, he says. At The Basic School nearly three hundred hours over the six months are set aside for captain-instructors to break off with small groups of second lieutenants specifically for the purpose of sharing such stories. "The captains here tell stories about Liberia, the majors about Desert Storm," says Lee. "Put something in a lecture or a handout or a book, and the student might or might not remember it. But put it in the context of the U.S. embassy burning down in Pakistan, and he'll remember." Call it an oral, informal case study method in which people's lives are staked on the outcome.

PRINCIPLE #11: BREED DECISIONMAKING BY ANALOGY

MBA VERSUS TBS

Some top business schools provide experiences that in many ways resemble those of both OCS and TBS. Students who have attended the Harvard or Stanford MBA program, for example, often speak of the initial shock of the daunting workloads, the fear of being washed out at the end of the first year, the teamwork-based exercises, the tight bonding between classmates, the entry into a vast network of graduates, and the teaching of case studies that can be applied to novel situations.

But there are also critical differences. Business school students may end up bonding with one another and becoming part of a strong culture, but the bonding and culture have nothing to do with the organization they'll end up in. They can't be brought into alignment with their corporate mission because they'll end up at businesses with different missions. And they have no opportunity to experience hands-on leadership until they're already working in organizations where early failures may not be regarded in a tolerant light. In fact MBA graduates are often regarded as talented but somewhat cynical hired guns who measure any situation in terms of what they can get out of it and are almost expected to be always looking around for a better deal. The result is that businesses that want to develop highly motivated, dedicated, and innovative managers can't count on MBA programs to impart these qualities; they have to find a way to nurture them in new managers.

One company that has made an effort to bridge the gap is General Electric, which spends $800 million a year on training and sends 5,000 managers a year through an intensive course in Crotonville, New York. CEO Jack Welch makes a point of lecturing extensively at the school and has claimed to spend at least two hours with 1,000 managers a year at the school's bar. Intel is no slouch in this regard either: it spent $312 million on training in 1998 and requires senior managers to teach four or more classes annually.

OBSESSIVE LEARNING

The formal education of business managers generally ends when they earn their MBAs. As much as Marines value on-the-job training and the education imparted by their MBA-program equivalent, The Basic School, they also believe that management is such a complex art and science that an officer's classroom education should continue throughout his or her career. By the time a Marine officer becomes a general, normally he or she will have attended at least four full-time schools after The Basic School, each one lasting an average of a year.

The schools, matched to particular levels in the hierarchy, move in primary focus from the tactical (lieutenants and captains) to the operational (captains, majors, and colonels) to the strategic (colonels and generals). In this section, I describe three of the major schools an officer might attend in a full, distinguished career. Not all officers would attend these particular schools, which are considered, to varying degrees, the more elite schools. Officers not destined to be promoted are less likely to be assigned to them. In addition, even officers earmarked for promotion might attend different Marine schools, schools of the other military branches, or even schools of a foreign military service. In fact being sent to a school run by a different military branch or service is considered an especially elite assignment, even though the officer has to make up all the material he or she will have missed at the Marine equivalent school on his or her own time via correspondence course.

Amphibious Warfare School

A nine-month school for only 205 captains, the Amphibious Warfare School is headed by Colonel Richard Barry, who calls amphibious warfare "the heart and soul of the Marine Corps." Being picked for AWS is the first major sign given to a Marine officer that he or she has been earmarked for a long career in the Marines: 80 percent of those who attend AWS will stay in the Corps at least twenty years. Much of the school time is spent in tactical decision exercises: after taking two minutes to read a scenario, a student must brief an instructor and a group of a dozen fellow students on how he or she would deal with it; that response is then critiqued by faculty and students. The topics covered may include how to mine a harbor, what happens if the battalion commander is killed, or what to do if a beach-landing party encounters unexpected opposition. Needless to say, there are no right answers. "We train for certainty and educate for uncertainty," says Barry, adding that 25 percent of the students' time is spent in the field. Among the guest speakers are a Holocaust survivor, an MIT professor who specializes in how people behave in battle, and a medical-school professor who studies teamwork. Field trips include a tour of a UPS facility to gain an appreciation of a finely tuned logistics operations.

Command and Staff College

Only one out of five majors are selected for this school, in which students are broken down into "conference groups" of sixteen, including at least one Army, one Air Force, and one foreign military student. Each group is mentored by both a high-ranking officer and a civilian professor of history, political science, or American studies. Students study command practices and the evolution of maneuver warfare, but the real emphasis is on examining historical and hypothetical war scenarios. The goal is to train students in analyzing situations when faced with incomplete, too much, or contradictory information and then distilling a clear briefing that will be useful to a high-level commander. Students must decide, for example, what Major General Sir William Howe should have reported to the king of England when he took over command of the English forces in America in 1775. "We're trying to give majors a framework to judge situations in a variety of contexts," says Colonel Darrell Browning, who helps direct the school. "We want them to winnow out the unimportant and find the nugget of information that will solve the problem." (If it seems inefficient to have professional soldiers taking time to study history and politics, consider that AT&T, Motorola, and other companies now have anthropologists on staff to help managers develop deeper insights into consumer behavior.)

Marine Corps War College

Also known as "McWar," this school is one of the most prestigious high-level military institutions in the world. It is here that a mere thirteen lieutenant colonels—one out of ten who are eligible—are prepared for the responsibility of a major command. Most will eventually become generals, and virtually all will be important Marine leaders. Moving beyond operational to strategic points of view, War College students study the history, culture, economy, and leadership of historical and current enemies in order to become skilled at identifying an opposing nation's leverage points, or "center of gravity"—that is, the factors that its leaders depend on to remain in power and that most affect a population's will to fight. Senators, cabinet members, influential reporters, and every three-star general in the Marine Corps drop in for guest lectures. Field trips include a visit to all five warfighting CINCs (commanders in chief)—the U.S. military command headquarters for the major regions of the world. Every graduate must put in a year as a War College faculty adviser.

The Corps doesn't rely solely on its system of schools to develop management talent. The process of turning a Marine into a leader has roots in virtually every routine practice in the organization, beginning when a man or woman walks into a Marine recruiting office and continuing until that Marine leaves the Corps. In the next chapter, we examine the different aspects of that process.

5. DEVELOPING MANAGERS

Sergeant Major Bill Whaley is of average height and build, except that his body appears to be made of hard plastic. He has a round face and generous features, and there's not a hint of stubble on his skull below a six-inch circle of hair that's so short it looks painted on.

"I was not that good a Marine when I came in," he recounts. "I was a crowd follower, always getting in trouble. Then one day a gunny [gunnery sergeant—a relatively high-ranking sergeant] pulled me aside and told me he was going to give me a recipe for promotion. 'You're not a ranting and raving guy,' he said. 'You're not a false motivation guy, you're not an every-time-you-see-'em-hurrah kind of guy. You are a deliberate, no-nonsense person, and don't try to be anything else.' He put me in positions where I could practice, be successful the first time out, and then get a harder challenge. He made me a senior driver for a high-explosive area. Then he made me responsible for security in the area. I made corporal. Then I became a corporal of the guard, then a sergeant of the guard. As soon as I became proficient at something, he'd find me something harder.

"That gunny, he saw something in me no one saw in me in my first nineteen years of life. When I told my stepfather I joined the Marine Corps, he said to me, 'You'll never make it,' and it was downhill from there. Now I challenge my sergeants with this: 'Is there a Lance Corporal Whaley in your unit? Can you find him?'"

Like most Marine officers and enlisted officers, Whaley understands that he has been entrusted not merely with making decisions but with personal responsibility for nurturing talent in younger officers who may someday take his place. That's just one of the many ways in which the Corps has embedded the development of management talent in both its formal and informal practices.

RECRUITING

After Logistics Colonel J. B. Beavers graduated from college and was accepted to law school in the late 1960s, he decided to take a break from academics and try a short spell in military service. His father had been in the Navy, so Beavers figured that would work for him, too. But the Navy recruiter, eyeing Beavers's educational credentials, pressed him to sign up not as an enlisted man but as an officer. The Navy needed men like him as officers, the recruiter told him; he would do well in Officer Candidate School and emerge with the privilege of being an officer in the U.S. Navy, with all its impressive responsibilities.

But Beavers didn't want to be an officer or go to any kind of school; he was trying to spend time *away* from school and responsibilities. Put off by the Navy recruiter's full-court press, he left and on a whim stopped in at a nearby Marine recruiting office. Before the Marine recruiter could mention anything about Beavers's options, Beavers told the man flat out that he had no interest in being an officer. "Just as well," said the recruiter. "You'd probably have a pretty hard time getting through Officer Candidate School." Beavers signed up on the spot as an officer candidate. "That guy really got my ass," he explains.

The Marines make it clear that they aren't as impressed with college degrees as the other services are. They're looking for something more in their officer candidates—something that, they're quick to imply, you as a candidate very well may lack. And that's exactly why the Marines attract so many top-notch candidates. One young man I spoke with had an MBA and a good job with the Commerce Department in international trade when he started talking to a Marine recruiter and was bitten by the "Am I good enough?" bug. Now a Marine lieutenant, he hopes to be a career officer.

I DARE YOU TO TAKE THIS JOB

Robert Young, CEO of the operating-system vendor Red Hat Software, reportedly spent his first interview with the lead candidate for the job of president explaining why the man would be crazy to accept a job that would put him directly up against Microsoft. The candidate is now the president.

The challenge of making officer isn't meant to appeal only to the best-educated Marines; nearly one-fifth of officer candidates are enlisted men and women who have decided to try to become commissioned officers. The Corps prides itself on the variety in background of its officers, recognizing that it needs field and even street smarts every bit as much as it needs book smarts in its decisionmakers.

PROMOTING

It's probably not surprising to hear that a Marine who refuses to obey a clear and legitimate order can face severe disciplinary action. What may be surprising is the fact that the officer who gave the order may find his or her own career stopped short over the same incident—even if the order was perfectly well advised. That's because the Marines have emphasized a simple, Darwinian test as part of determining an officer's suitability for promotion: Is he or she someone who inspires people to follow?

It's not that all Marine officers are charismatic people revered by subordinates (though a significant percentage are). Plenty of popular officers are washed out along the way because they didn't succeed in getting their people to stretch. Likewise, some high-level Marine leaders are entirely unremarkable in bearing and don't garner great affection from the Marines they command. They've made it to the top, however, because, for whatever reasons, when they ask people to do the seemingly impossible, those people give it everything they have and impressive things get done.

Promotion decisions are made by centralized formal boards composed of cream-of-the-crop officers who are rotated onto the board for a tour of duty (which, as we see later, is in keeping with the Marine philosophy on personnel issues). The decision is based on feedback from other Marine officers who have supervised and observed the promotion candidate—feedback that heavily reflects the responsiveness the candidate earned from the people under him or her.

The Corps has no problem finding enough officers worthy of promotion. On the contrary, it turns out too many top-notch officers at most levels to allow for moving *all* of the successful ones to the next level in the hierarchy. The filter is especially opaque at the top end: only one in sixteen colonels are destined to make general.

The Corps is quite frank with its officers from the outset about the statistical unlikelihood of steady promotion. Actually, they're given even worse news than that: at any level up through major, a Marine who is not promoted is forced out of active duty. Colonels do not have to make general to remain in the Corps). The first hurdle hits fast. When Marines leave The Basic School, it has been spelled out for them that, barring a strong performance on their part, they will be leaving the Corps (at least as an active duty officer) in thirty months. The winnowing out of officers—even good ones—is relentless in the Corps, and it happens not just when an officer is up for promotion but also when he or she is competing for the high-profile assignments that tend to lead to promotion, such as positions of command and tours as students or instructors at the top schools.

THE SECRET CEILING

The narrow gauntlet of promotion is a fact of life at many, if not most, organizations. But companies tend to treat the poor odds of moving up as a dirty secret; even the weakest managers operate under the belief that they're likely to work their way up. When they don't, they feel betrayed by their supervisors and by the organization. The epidemic of disgruntled employees in the United States has many causes, but surely the false and ultimately shattered hope of promotion is one of the major ones. One exception: GE's promotion policy requires that all managers be regularly given a numerical grade. Those who receive a middling ranking have no illusions about promotion, and those given a lower ranking know they will be asked to leave the company.

How does the Corps keep officers from stressing out or becoming disheartened over the daunting odds against being allowed to make a career out of the Marines? "We freely talk about it, give them the expectation that most don't make it, and make sure they understand that not getting selected doesn't mean they're not a good officer," says Lehockey. "We teach them to not worry about what they can't control. Marines learn to bloom where planted, and if they do the very best with the job they're given, then everything else will take care of itself."

The intense competition for promotion would almost certainly lead to a cutthroat environment among managers in most organizations. But in the Marines the drive to move ahead of other officers is overwhelmed by the cultural mandate to be supportive. "We want to be better than our fellow Marines, but not at their expense," says one colonel. "When I was a company commander in a rifle battalion, if one of us got chewed out by the colonel, the first thing we'd do was get on the phone and warn the other two not to make the same mistake."

Another potential drawback to the "up or out" situation for Marine officers is the possibility that some of the very best officers leave the Corps on their own in part because they are unsure of their long-term prospects. Since decisions are made by ever-changing promotion boards, there is no one who can sit down with such an officer and guarantee him or her a sure ride to the top. But the Corps does have a way of getting the message across. Certain types of assignments are considered critical to making it as far as colonel, and even more so to achieving the rank of general. These high-profile positions include postings within recruiting; as an instructor or commander of instructors; as a student in an officers' school run by another branch of the military; as a student in one of the elite officers' schools; as an infantry commander (all the more impressive if during an active major conflict); as an executive officer (second in command); as a "monitor" (career counselor); as a battalion commander; and to a high-visibility security post, a promotion board, or Marine headquarters at the Pentagon.

An officer at any level who receives one of these golden assignments is getting a signal from the Corps that he or she is being set up for the next level. If the golden assignments continue throughout his or her career, then the message is even clearer: you are being fast-tracked for a climb to the top.

Consider the résumé to date of Colonel Rick Zilmer, the officer who received the unnerving send-off from his recruiter on the bus to OCS. The résumé begins with his commissioning as a second lieutenant in 1974, followed by the following positions: company executive officer at boot camp, student at the Army's infantry officers' course, captain of a rifle company sent to Beirut, security officer at Camp David, instructor at The Basic School, student at Command Staff College, infantry battalion executive officer, operations officer for the lead force in the Gulf War, monitor, student at the Naval War College, infantry battalion commander, senior U.S. exchange officer to the British Royal Marines, and MEU commander. In the Marines compiling this sort of résumé is as close as one gets to formal grooming to be a general.

Not all colonels and generals can point back to a series of elite stints, but most can. Of course, such stints are a two-edged sword. Though they aid in moving up to the next level, they are also extremely difficult to excel at; failing at any one posting to do anything less would probably put a long, distinguished career out of the picture. But the fact that the Corps demands high performance at these critical slots ensures that top Marine leaders have been put through the most stringent of filters and have received the ultimate in preparation.

A Marine officer who isn't promoted and who thus must leave active duty isn't necessarily ending his or her career with the Corps. Marines who exercise their option of becoming reservists may be on active duty anywhere from one to six months per year. "There's no patch anywhere on my uniform that indicates I'm different in any way from any other Marine," one reserve colonel told me. (At Microsoft, in contrast, permanent employees wear blue patches to distinguish them from orange-patched contract or part-time employees, who don't receive full benefits or stock options.) Some officers who leave are offered the opportunity to become civilian employees of the Marines, sometimes in important positions as administrative, policy-advising, or research managers. I spoke to one successful major who had been a lieutenant, left the Corps, missed it, signed back up as an enlisted Marine, went to boot camp, then went on to OCS, and this time quickly moved up the ladder.

No Marine is ever regarded as having truly "left" the Corps, and the number of officers who make the transition to civilian life carrying hard feelings appears to be remarkably low.

THE PLUG-AND-PLAY MANAGER

In the business world a company might make a point of having managers sit on assembly lines or take customer complaints a few days a year, or it might shift marketing specialists to a different product line now and again. Marine officers, no matter what their expertise, can expect over the course of a career to perform several tours of duty in positions entirely outside that area. Infantry commanders are placed in charge of supply brigades, and Marine lawyers—called judge advocate generals, or JAGs—are given infantry units to command. One sergeant told me he had been a jet-engine mechanic before moving into a slot as information technology manager at a Marine school, where he now spends his time developing websites and building computer networks. It's a typical story.

In the short term, concedes Colonel Lee, this almost random-seeming shuffling around robs an organization of the efficiencies that would be obtained by allowing people to develop better skills in one job. In the long term, though, the organization gains, he says, because it has developed a body of plug-and-play managers capable of joining any team in almost any role in response to almost any crisis. Providing a lawyer with infantry training may seem like an exercise in inefficiency, but the Marine JAGs sent to Kosovo to mediate residents' disputes at the start of the post-bombing NATO occupation probably treasured every moment of that training.

PRINCIPLE #12: CROSS-TRAIN

The shuffling around, of course, is not entirely random. For one thing, there are certain rough rules of rotation: a captain's first tour of duty, for example, is with the fleet (that is, with frontline troops or the units that support them), and the second tour is likely to involve administrative, personnel, or school-related duties. Similarly, majors are generally given staff rather than command jobs.

But in most cases the Corps' monitors—the group of top-notch officers at Marine headquarters who serve as traffic directors for Marine careers—make job assignments by trying to balance the Corps' needs for talent in particular areas with each officer's best interests.

If the needs conflict, those of the Corps win out. As we discuss later, some of the most gung-ho Marines are firmly plunked down for two or more years in personnel-related jobs for which they would never have signed up. (The intensely paperwork-heavy and stressful job of monitor itself, fittingly enough, is one of the best examples.) And there are few people who enter the Marines and go through the rigors of boot camp or OCS in order to be public relations specialists. But the Corps places a high value on how it's viewed by the nation, and so its public affairs offices are staffed by highly regarded Marines who are usually putting in a tour of duty in the function at the Corps' (non-negotiable) request.

The Corps policy of shuffling people between positions is not primarily a means of filling the less popular slots. It's done more for the good of the officers. Part of the reasoning is that if managers understand how other departments function, and thus how the organization as a whole functions, they can manage their own group in a way that makes a better contribution to the organization. "A Marine officer might think of himself as a steely-eyed infantryman, but he's got to understand supply operations," says Colonel Beavers.

Sergeant Major Joseph Gentelia, the senior enlisted officer of a service and support group, notes that the constant moving around also rounds out management skill sets that might otherwise be lopsided if developed solely in one specialty. "Each job has unique personnel problems," he says, "and each time you're exposed to a new problem the more of a leader you become." What's more, being thrown into new positions without specific preparation is valuable training in its own right. "When I was first transferred into logistics, the person I was replacing was gone already, and there was a gunny temporarily filling in for him," he recalls. "I was a little scared, so I asked the gunny if I could watch him for a week. The second day I asked him to clear his stuff out. Now I tell that story to all new first sergeants. At first you depend on the black-and-white rules and procedures, but as you get more experience you learn better ways to get it done."

As Beavers puts it: "With everyone transferring around, there's no stagnation. I had an executive officer from a landing support group taken away for 179 days. I could moan and groan about it, but a young major or captain or sergeant gets sent in to fill the gap, he's thrown into the breach. If he screws up, I say, 'Okay, now you know.' And that's how training happens."

None of this is to suggest that the Corps doesn't recognize the value of specialization. Marine officers typically do have specialties, even if they're occasionally pulled away from them. Brigadier General Paul Lee has been primarily a logistician for nearly three decades, for example. And pilots tend to stay pilots, with a few outside tours thrown in, until they're experienced enough to command other pilots.

TRAINING THE SUPERVISORS

There's really no close analogy in business management to the Marines' parallel management tracks of commissioned officers (lieutenants, captains, majors, colonels, and generals) and noncommissioned, or enlisted, officers (corporals and sergeants). Put roughly, commissioned officers decide what their unit is going to do, and enlisted officers provide advice and supervise the enactment of those orders. Though technically speaking a top-ranking sergeant—a master sergeant—with twenty years of experience is outranked by the greenest second lieutenant fresh out of OCS, in practice the higher-level sergeants wield vast influence and command tremendous respect from Marines of all ranks.

The enlisted officers' ranks might be seen as a separate management track for employees who, by virtue of experience and skill, are capable of taking on the additional responsibilities of management but aren't interested in moving too far away from the frontline aspects of the job. (Some younger enlisted officers actually do end up setting their sights on winning a commission, and those who succeed are accorded the highest respect. In fact the top graduate of many an Officer Candidate School class is a former enlisted officer.)

INSIDE OPPORTUNITIES AND ACCIDENTAL CROSS-TRAINING

A number of companies have made a policy of nurturing management skills in the lowest ranks. Solectron, an electronics manufacturer in Milpitas, California, promoted nearly one-quarter of its West Coast workers in 1998. McDonald's Corporation is also noted for the opportunity it provides its rank-and-file workers. Robert Beavers started at the company as a $1-an-hour part-time worker behind the counter and eventually became a senior vice president and board member before resigning his posts in 1999 to help take a Campbell Soup Company division private.

In terms of cross-training, few businesses are as obsessive about it as the Corps—and fast-growing technology companies generally give no thought to it whatsoever, given their typically short-term focus and high employee turnover rates, reported to average about 30 percent a year among Silicon Valley Internet firms. Interestingly enough, however, some observers have argued that Silicon Valley and other high-tech business communities serve as aggregate cross-training platforms because managers learn different skills as they shuffle from one company to the next. Perhaps, but it seems unlikely that this sort of potluck cross-training could be counted on to provide the benefits of a more thoughtfully monitored effort.

As with commissioned officers, the Marines take the development of enlisted officers seriously, offering training programs for each of the seven levels of ranks. Entry-level sergeants, for example, who are essentially commanders for a squad of about twelve Marines, take an intense five-week course that includes training in writing, navigating urban combat, medivacking injured, calling for air and artillery strikes, researching foreign cultures, monitoring evacuations, managing a squad's weapons and other equipment, and training corporals.

The school for the next level up, staff sergeants, is far more demanding. Staff sergeants assist lieutenants in running platoons of thirty-five or so people, and that assistance is regarded as critical by the Marines. "The lieutenant is probably twenty-three years old, has been in the Marine Corps for a year, and has seen things operate under ideal conditions," says Sergeant Major Whaley. "The staff sergeant has been in for four to six years, has had two tours of duty, including a couple of floats, has faced real problems and made decisions with real consequences, and has seen things operate under the worst conditions."

Whaley should know: he runs the sergeants' programs at Quantico. (Virtually all the enlisted-officer training programs are run by enlisted officers.) "Our school operates at half the budget of the next-least-funded school at Quantico," he says proudly, employing the calm, soft-spoken manner of a person with huge reserves of both self-confidence and humility. While I'm talking with him in his office, one general with whom Whaley used to work calls to ask his opinion on a personnel matter. It's not unusual for generals to call him, he says. "We're mutually supportive," he explains.

I observe Whaley addressing a new class of staff sergeants at the school. Most of these men and women look like formidable characters, but Whaley instantly has them mesmerized; the fact that he speaks so quietly seems to add to the force of his words. He tells them to let him know if they ever have any ideas on how to make the school better. "Besides being dark, my skin is pretty darn thick," he says. "Don't just tell me what's broken, tell me how to fix it. If you don't feel you've been treated like a staff sergeant, or with the respect due any Marine, or unprofessionally in any way, don't stand on formality. Come and tell me. You'll see me every day. And I guarantee you you'll see me at PT." PT is Marine-speak for physical training. Though Marines don't spend nearly as much time on conditioning as the public might assume—three hours a week is typical—it is always ferocious, and schools like this one step up the frequency and intensity.

Later Whaley, who is some two decades older than most of the students, admits to me that the PT is hard on him. That's because he participates in all the PT sessions at both the sergeants' and staff sergeants' schools lest either group think that he favors one over the other or that he considers himself too high up for PT. As tough as the PT is at staff sergeants' school, though, the program is not about physical fitness. In addition to learning advanced and expanded versions of the material from the sergeants' course, plus much of what lieutenants learn, the staff sergeants will also be given broader perspectives on the nature of war. They will travel to Washington, D.C., for example, to visit the Holocaust Museum.

Whaley tells me that he believes the impression he personally makes on the students is critical to the ambitions they'll have in their own careers. "It's not important that they remember my name," he says. "It's just important that when they first look at me they think, 'Oh, so that's what a sergeant major looks like. They must be pretty good.'"

Whaley believes that his own success is strictly due to his having been on the receiving end of that sort of inspiration and attention. The story he tells at the beginning of this chapter is similar to those I hear from a surprising number of Marines, including colonels and even generals. Whaley practices what he preaches. He heard about a private who went AWOL for three months before finally showing up at Quantico. Whaley offered to take him on. "He's from a poor, dour situation," he explains. "He's the son of a single parent, there's nothing for him back home. I looked at him as a great challenge and opportunity. I made him an administrative clerk here. I took him to the sergeant majors' annual picnic, and I had his picture taken with the sergeant major of the Marine Corps. I told him, 'That's your legacy.' I can't put heart into him, but if the heart's there, maybe I can put the desire into him."

CONTINUING THE PROCESS

The development of management skills among Marine officers doesn't happen only in schools and training programs. Marine officers and enlisted officers are constantly working with the officers under them to refine their understanding of various leadership practices and philosophies. Here are three of the most important ideas that Marine leaders try to get across to their subordinates.

KEEP MANAGERS FOCUSED ON THE LOWEST RANKS

A phrase that Marine officers and enlisted officers hear over and over is, "You work for your people." "People" applies to all Marines, including direct subordinates, but the emphasis is on the frontline Marine. Says Sergeant Major Gentelia: "The most important thing an enlisted officer can do is make sure the junior enlisted leaders are doing the right things by their Marines, that they're treating each Marine firmly, fairly, and with dignity. I look at every set of discharge papers and try to see if that Marine's supervisors were short on patience. I'm especially suspicious if I see that the Marine had been doing well for a long time and then suddenly his work was unsatisfactory. I'll call his supervisor in and ask, 'Are you sure you did everything you could to make this Marine as excellent as possible?'" Gentelia has good reason to believe in the redemptive potential of all Marines: he himself was court-martialed as a corporal and reduced in rank, but he ended up landing coveted DI and recruiter positions, eventually making it to the highest enlisted officer rank.

GROOM YOUR REPLACEMENT

Marine officers and enlisted officers insist that they work at least as hard on developing their number-two person's capabilities as they do their own. To some extent, this philosophy is simply a form of mentoring: though officers are expected to help all their people progress, showering extra attention on a particular subordinate helps ensure that key talent can move up even more quickly and that all of a more senior officer's insights and skills are transferred to the organization.

But it also reflects the straightforward reality that Marine leaders can be killed, incapacitated, or suddenly moved to another position and that the Marines can't afford gross discontinuities in leadership. Says General Steele: "If you want to judge the depth of an organization, then remove a key leader and watch what happens. You've got to have a backup, and a third bench, too. You want it to be second nature for your people to pick up leadership when the need arises."

MANAGEMENT BACKUP

One indication of the failure of most businesses to nurture backup talent comes from a survey conducted by Management Recruiters International revealing that four out of five executives continue to run the show to some extent while they're on vacation. Some executives wisely take pains, however, to go in the opposite direction: management depth is built, they believe, when they take a long vacation out of contact with the company. Matt Simmons, president of the investment bank Simmons & Company, reportedly said when he let go of the reins for a two-month vacation: "If the firm still works fine, then you probably have a second generation in place." America Online CEO Steve Case, who has been praised for his willingness to stay in the background, has asserted: "If I resigned tomorrow, AOL would go on. If Bill Gates resigned tomorrow, people would be shocked."

CULTIVATE A UNIQUE STYLE

Organizations often have a way of expelling, grinding down, or remolding managers who don't conform to the personal style favored by the organization, be it brash, conservative, or laid-back. Marine officers, in contrast, exhibit a hugely variegated collection of styles that defy categorization. One thing officers do have in common is that the Corps isn't interested in *changing* their personal style—only in finding ways to make that style work better for them. Says Barry: "If there's a right way to manage, then how can a screaming Bear Bryant and a reserved Bud Wilkinson both be such effective coaches?" Or, as Colonel Robert Lee puts it: "If you're not a Patton, you shouldn't act like one."

Officers and enlisted officers at all levels are encouraged to work at refining their insight into their own style, assessing all their weaknesses and strengths, and as they get a handle on it to spell it right out for subordinates. Higher-level officers publicly post a written description of their style as one of their first actions in taking over a command position. These range from short paragraphs with a string of curt sentences such as, "I won't micromanage, but attention to detail is important," to seven-page manifestos. "As a commander, you need to let people know who you're dealing with," says Colonel Henry Browning. "I was a commander of a helicopter squadron and air group, and I told everyone I'm anal-retentive, a Felix Unger. If you know what your limitations are, you can compensate and warn people. As things change, they can guess where you'd go with it and can accomplish the mission without requiring your micromanaging. They understand your intent better if they understand you."

No matter how proficient an organization's managers are, the job won't get done without the frontline people. In the next two chapters, we examine how the Corps applies its leaders' skills to bring out the best in their Marines—so that the mission gets accomplished every time.

6. DIRECTING PEOPLE

A sergeant has assigned two young privates the task of painting the hallways in a small building. The privates are wielding their buckets and brushes, ready for their instructions. The sergeant calls them over to a corner of the corridor and points to a section of the wall where the color from the old paint is streaked and hardened paint-drips line the wood trim near the floor. "Look at this," he says, as the privates lean over. "This right here is crummy painting." Then he walks ten feet over to a doorway, beckons to the men, and indicates the area around the door. "This is an excellent paint job. Look at the attention to detail here. This is the difference between a good paint job and a bad paint job. Do you understand the difference?" The privates peer at the door, and then say they get it. "Good," says the sergeant. "Okay. Good luck." The sergeant disappears. Two hours later the privates are still painting carefully and efficiently. The sergeant won't drop in on them for a while longer, and when he does, he'll pronounce the work "outstanding" before pointing out a few places that need a little retouching.

Painting corridors may not seem like an exciting venue in which to put Marine management principles to the test. But the interaction between the sergeant and the privates illustrates some of the key elements of how Marine managers keep their people motivated and get their best efforts, even when the work doesn't have the inherent challenge or thrill of storming a beach. Specifically, the sergeant didn't tell the men exactly how to perform their job; he simply made clear the results he was looking for. He didn't micromanage them; instead, his absence indicated his trust. He made a point of declaring their job a success, building their confidence and giving them a sense of mission accomplished. And rather than raking them over the coals for their errors, he gave them constructive criticism so that they would know that, as good a job as they did, the Corps' high standards demand that next time they will do even better. The results: the two privates came away feeling that once again they were able to do what it takes and that their work was appreciated; the sergeant got a first-rate paint job and the continued enthusiasm of two Marines to excel at whatever tasks the Corps throws at them.

Of the many things that officers and enlisted officers are expected to get right in the Corps, providing direction in a way that guides employees without restricting them is considered one of the most crucial. It's a skill that Marines work on throughout their careers.

WHAT TO DO, NOT HOW TO DO IT

The essence of the Marine style of giving direction is to avoid telling someone exactly how to do things when giving orders. Instead, Marine officers provide two clear statements: first, how they would like the situation to end up, what the Marines refer to as "the end state"; and second, the broader goals that they would like to achieve through the entire unit's actions, information that Marines call "the commander's intent."

PRINCIPLE #13: MANAGE BY END STATE AND INTENT

End state and intent are critical concepts for the Marines because they leave the details of execution up to the doer. If a corporal wants a private to stack a bunch of pallets, he won't tell him to get a forklift, or to grab two other privates; he'll simply tell him to make sure the pallets get stacked. Marines give instructions like these because, in an environment where events are unfolding quickly and unpredictably, a particular means to an end can suddenly become unfeasible, but if the end is well understood, then other means can be enlisted.

Managers at most organizations prefer to spell out exactly how they want an employee to accomplish a task because not doing so carries the sometimes considerable risk that the employee will carry it out in an inefficient or even disastrous fashion. This is a trade-off the Marines make consciously. "I give them the mission and get the hell out of their way," says Bedard. "If I have to tell a guy how to do something from A to Z, then I don't need him. We use trust tactics: if you tell me you're going to do it, then I trust that you will, and you'll trust me that I've given you the right mission."

Marines do equip their people with specific information about how to perform various types of actions; in fact Marines are provided with a vast wealth of knowledge about practices and procedures. But these specifics serve as a foundation on which on-the-fly decision-making is built, not a detailed prescription for dealing with the surprises of the real world. Such rigid prescriptions are sometimes useful for dealing with purely mechanical tasks—field-stripping a rifle, for example. But even then, Marines are taught to be prepared to break the rules and improvise; rifles too, after all, can fail in surprising ways. When it comes to dealing with scenarios controlled by people who have wills of their own, explicit instructions can become almost useless.

THE PROBLEM WITH RULES

Why do so many businesses that claim to be obsessed with customer satisfaction—or customer *delight,* as the latest trend dictates—manage to hugely irritate a significant percentage of their customers? The frontline people who are typically the vehicle of customer annoyance often seem to be perfectly intelligent, moderately trained, reasonably dedicated employees. They appear to believe that they are acting in the company's interests when they refuse to authorize a refund, decline to fulfill a special request, or insist that they can't retrieve a needed piece of information.

Yet it's hard to believe that higher-level managers at these companies wouldn't want these frontline employees to handle such situations differently so as to ensure that the interaction ends with a satisfied customer, at small cost to the business.

The problem, I believe, is that managers tend to rely on giving employees explicit rules about how to handle various situations. No matter how clever the rules are, however, or how many of them are disseminated, they will never adequately cover all the situations an employee is likely to face. McDonald's, for example, is famous for having refined a set of processes and rules in which new employees are thoroughly drilled. And yet virtually every time I'm in line at McDonald's I notice one of the frenetically working servers being thrown off-stride by a situation that no one ever warned him or her about: a homeless person who wants to know whether she can have half a cup of coffee for half-price; a batch of milk-shake mix that's coming out a funny color; or a customer who needs to know whether there are any animal products in the salad. Line delays, meanwhile, are one of the biggest sources of annoyance to McDonald's customers, a fact to which almost any parent can attest. The solution isn't to add more rules. Rules are the problem.

One manager who avoids spelling things out for his people is GE's Welch, who has reportedly said that the only direction he gives his subordinates is "to grow this company as fast as we can."

Colonel Schmidle, who helped run the Camp Lejeune invasion exercise described in chapter 2, suggests that the concepts of end state and intent jibe well with chaos theory. "You can't predict the exact behavior of a complex system," he explains, "but there are ways to understand how the system is likely to end up." In other words, you can't choose which sequence of events will lead to a given result, but that doesn't mean you can't choose the result; you just have to leave open an infinite number of paths for getting there.

As an example, Schmidle describes the commander's intent given to some of the Marines who took part in the Lejeune exercises: don't let the Landrone insurgency leader organize a counterattack. "I didn't tell them to do it by cutting off someone's head or cutting off someone's communications," he says. "I just told them to deny the Landrones the leadership. If a Marine sees the opportunity to accomplish that intent, he'll do it, even if he doesn't have the opportunity to get the orders to do it." (Incidentally, the streets at Marine bases are typically named after important Marine battles and concepts. Fittingly enough, the mock battle at Camp Lejeune lapped up to the edge of End State Road.)

The Marines employ intent and end state throughout the chain of command. At the top of the chain, commanding generals are acting on end states and intents that have been provided by the Pentagon and may take months to be realized. As orders are passed down through the layers, the intents and end states become more focused and are applied to missions of shorter time spans. At the bottom of the chain, squads and platoons are acting on intents and end states that may apply for a day or even a few hours. But the goal of the intent and end state articulated at each level is to help achieve the intent and end state of the level above it. In this way, the broad, strategic end states and intents of the top commanders essentially trickle down into the thousands of end states and intents directing frontline Marines.

THE MAIN EFFORT AND RULES OF ENGAGEMENT

There are two other concepts that Marine officers rely on when giving out mission orders: the main effort and the rules of engagement. Typically an officer provides three sets of mission orders, one to each of his or her subordinate units. (For example, a captain commanding a company will give mission orders to each of the three lieutenants commanding a platoon in the company.) Each mission will come with an end state that is usually tailored to that mission and a commander's intent that, being broader in scope, may cover all three. But the officer will also normally make it clear to all three units receiving the orders that one of the missions has been designated "the main effort."

Often the main effort is simply the most important of the three missions, the one whose success or failure will have the greatest impact on the end state and intent of the next level up the chain. The units that know their mission is a "supporting effort"—that it's not the main effort—can use that information to take actions that may even hurt the chances of their own mission succeeding but contribute to the success of the main effort. If, for example, a unit assigned to manning a roadblock near a threatened embassy is aware that the main effort lies with the unit protecting the gates of the embassy, the first unit will know to abandon the roadblock and reinforce the gate-protection unit if a firefight breaks out in front of the embassy. "It's a scheme for prioritization," says Captain Brendon McBreen. "It helps avoid situations where you do your job but the organization fails."

But a mission need not be more important than others to be tagged a main effort. If three missions are essentially equal in importance, then one can be arbitrarily designated the main effort. That way, if one or more units become overwhelmed, they know to collapse back on the main effort in the hopes that the combined strength of the units will do at least the one job. When three squads set up security around a perimeter, one will be named the main effort for that reason. What's more, the "main effort" designation can be fluid: if communications remain open, the commander or the subordinates themselves can redirect the main effort on the fly.

McBreen relates a possibly apocryphal sea story often told to Marines to bring home the importance of the concept of the main effort. During the Korean War three Marine platoons were given missions to take three different bridges over a river the Marines needed to cross. All three platoons—none of which were designated the main effort—were outgunned by enemy units defending the bridges, and ultimately all three failed to cross. But one bridge turned out to be slightly less well defended than the others, and the platoon that tried to take it came within inches of the far side before being driven back.

"If that platoon had been designated the main effort," explains McBreen, "the other two platoons would have joined it, and they would have taken the bridge."

The "rules of engagement," another component to orders, differ from end state, intent, and the main effort in that they apply to how missions are to be accomplished rather than to the results of the missions. In keeping with the principle of not telling subordinates how to complete their tasks, the rules of engagement don't tell Marines what to do; rather, they describe for Marines what, in general terms, they should try to *avoid* doing. In effect, the rules of engagement lay out boundary lines, or constraints, to the solutions that Marines can come up with in trying to complete a mission.

For example, Marines typically have a variety of tools to draw on when facing a threat, representing diminishing levels of deadliness. They can call in airstrikes to obliterate the threat; they can bring in tanks to run over it; they can shoot at it with rifles; they can spray mace at it; or they can try to talk their way out of it. The rules of engagement help Marines decide which levels they should rule out, or at least lean away from. Such rules are of particular importance when dealing with people as motivated as Marines. The rules of engagement help Marines keep their perspective on a situation so that, for example, they don't end up enlisting a means to success that ultimately causes a problem bigger than the one the mission was supposed to solve. As an example, Major General Bedard recounts a rule of engagement given to the Marines in Somalia: "If a vehicle approaches a roadblock and refuses to stop, standard operating procedure is to take the vehicle and all its occupants down," he says. "But what if you could see there were women and children in the vehicle? Then they had the option of just shooting out the tires."

A LACK OF LIMITS

When a business gets hammered by lawsuits from competitors or the Justice Department, or receives a stream of complaints from irate customers who feel they've been misled or oversold, or is constantly getting slammed in the press, it may be a sign that managers have been negligent in laying out clear and appropriate rules of engagement for employees—or even that senior managers fail to grasp the need for such rules. Microsoft would spring to many minds. During its antitrust trial convincing evidence was offered by a number of executives in the computer industry that Microsoft has routinely tried to sabotage the viability of new software approaches, even if doing so involved taking a loss and ultimately reducing the overall functionality of the software available to the world. Sun Microsystems executives testified, for example, that Microsoft attempted to stamp out the popular version of the Java programming language—whose enormous benefit is to allow programs to run on multiple software platforms—by flooding the market with a version of Java that worked only with its own software platforms.

THE CHALLENGE OF BEING NONPRESCRIPTIVE

Letting subordinates decide how to carry out tasks doesn't sound like much of a burden on managers, but in fact most managers are entirely unused to giving out "nonprescriptive" assignments. "It's not a natural way to give orders," says General Steele. "You have to drill yourself on it and recognize that things are going to be too fluid out there to do it any other way. It's better to have to rein your people in than to have to push them like a plow."

Schmidle notes that any uneasiness an officer feels when letting subordinates find their own path to mission completion is not irrational. "It means I incur a larger risk as a commander, because when I allow people to carry out orders as they see fit, messy stuff happens," he says. "There's a perception of a loss of control." Schmidle adds that he experienced that feeling himself during the Lejeune exercise.

"When we gave the commanders our intent, I had a mental image of how they would coordinate their fire," he recalls. "But they came up with something completely different. At first I thought, 'Oh, no, this isn't going to work.' Then I realized that if I had dictated to them what I had in mind, I would have gotten a predictable product. Surprise is a good thing, not a bad thing, and it takes a while to get comfortable with that."

PUSHING SMARTS DOWN

"If I were to compare Marines today to what I had in Vietnam," says Randy Gangle, "it would be night and day. Marines today have a better intellect, a better education, fewer discipline problems, and a different mental attitude. I was a regimental commander in Desert Storm, and I visited with those young soldiers before the invasion. They were quiet and focused. There was none of this 'I can't wait to kill a bunch of gooks' stuff. They were reviewing flash cards that helped identify the silhouettes of enemy equipment."

If Marines are going to exercise their own judgment in carrying out missions, they have to have the mental acuity, creativity, and knowledge to deal with fast-changing, complex situations. "More than ever, the Marines at the lower levels need to know more than just rote tasks," says one colonel. "The Marine's mind is becoming our main weapons system."

PRINCIPLE #14: DISTRIBUTE COMPETENCE

By all accounts, the Corps has succeeding in pushing smarts down to all ranks. "I have four Marines in my platoon with college degrees," says one infantry sergeant. "I have lance corporals who deal with $2 million pieces of electronic equipment. We start missions off by talking about when the ionosphere will be opening up so we can hit the birds."

Part of that success in raising the competence of even the lowest enlisted ranks is, of course, related to the top-notch job the Corps has done with recruiting. But a lot of it has to do with what the Corps does with people once they become Marines. The Corps has made an extraordinary effort to refine its lower-level training programs.

For starters, the Marines tap outstanding performers to fill instructor slots, regarded as one of the high-profile tours of duty. In addition, the training is essentially never-ending. Whether at peace or at war, Marines are constantly being pushed to learn new skills and to refine the old ones.

Much of the training has been revamped in recent years to emphasize growing intellectual demands. "In the 1970s we raised the intellectual standards of recruits," says Gangle, "but we didn't change our training style. We jumped from people with a sixth-grade education to people with high school diplomas, and they became bored with the training. In the 1980s we added in recon [reconnaissance] skills, and calling in artillery fire from naval and aviation, and they learned it in a heartbeat. Now we've ratcheted it up across the board. We think we're just basically catching up to their capabilities."

The demands of maneuver warfare and urban warfare have made such in-depth training essential. Gangle notes as an example that standard training teaches Marines to get over a "concertina," or sharpened-wire, fence by cutting it or throwing a log against it. But no one was teaching them the biggest danger about urban concertina fences: they're often erected to shepherd soldiers into an ambush. Not until urban warfare simulations like the one at Camp Lejeune resulted in Marines taking high "casualties" from such ambushes was it recognized that the troops needed to be shown the big picture. Gangle and his team threw together a two-hour training session in how to avoid urban ambushes, and casualty rates dropped 50 percent among Marines who took the session. "You have to recognize the fact that you don't know what you don't know," says Gangle.

Marine training is famous for being physically demanding, but more and more time is spent simply talking. During a daylong exercise the entire second half of the day is sometimes spent simply discussing what happened during the first half. Marines also learn to take the decisions they make during training very seriously. One sergeant told me that he had been ordered by his captain during an exercise to hunt down a guerrilla leader. The captain was clear with his end state: he wanted the leader dead, not taken prisoner, regardless of any efforts to surrender. The sergeant dutifully tracked the leader down and "shot" him, even though the man had thrown his arms in the air. "I knew killing someone who surrendered was an illegal act, but I figured, what the hell, it was an exercise," recalls the sergeant. When he reported back to his captain, he was thoroughly chewed out. "He told me, 'What you do in training is what you end up doing in real life.'" Since then the sergeant chews his own Marines out for even joking about illegal acts, never mind performing them in exercises.

One critical aspect of Marine training involves having every Marine learn the different elements to Marine warfare, regardless of his or specialty. "The Army guy will tell you about his Howitzer, the Navy guy about his submarine, the Air Force guy about his fighter jet," says Kirk Nicholas, a former Marine now employed by the Marines' Combat Development Group. "The Marine guy will tell you everything from air and artillery support to how to load a ship or fight with tanks. We even make aviators do ground tours with an infantry unit."

Cross-training helps Marines understand how their piece of the mission fits into the overall picture, and it reinforces the cultural emphasis on a shared Marine identity. But it also has a more tangible benefit: Marines can sometimes fill in for jobs other than their own if the need arises. Lieutenant Colonel John Allison notes that a lot of job-swapping took place in Mogadishu, Somalia, where the constraints of working among a dense population of civilians ruled out using artillery; artillery specialists ran patrols and performed other tasks instead. "Marines often get thrust into missions that don't call for standard preparation," says Allison. What's more, Marines are typically trained to perform not only multiple jobs at their level but also their boss's job, since the Corps doesn't want anyone to be hard to replace. In the business world managers are often resentful or fearful of employees who seem a little too eager to move up into their position. Marine officers demand that eagerness. "Every one of my Marines can do my job," boasts one sergeant.

The Corps also places a great emphasis on reading. Enlisted Marines are provided with a list of required and recommended books. In keeping with the principle of trying to have people be enthusiastic about the things they're ordered to do, the books are carefully selected both to reinforce important warfighting concepts and to be fun reads. Two of the most popular books on the list are modern science fiction classics: Orson Scott Card's *Ender's Game* and Robert Heinlein's *Starship Troopers*; both books feature combat scenarios in which initiative and inventiveness prove decisive. Another book, *Rifleman Dodd* by C. S. Forester of "Horatio Hornblower" fame, which tells the tale of an infantryman able to remain effective in the absence of direct orders, was so admired by Marines that the Corps bought the right to print up 220,000 copies, which it distributes to every single Marine. (In fact the book is now otherwise out of print.) More recently the Corps has been snatching up computer games that require making real-time strategic and tactical decisions, both for distributing to Marines who own PCs and for loading onto shared computers in recreation rooms.

A wider variety of Marines are also becoming more adept at making use of intelligence information. Traditionally, data about enemy strength, satellite maps, and other intelligence are given to higher-level officers, who parcel out whatever pieces of it are directly relevant to subordinates' missions. Precious little of it ends up filtering down to the lowest ranks who actually carry out the missions. Now the Marines are trying to make more data about the big picture available to lower-level leaders, in the belief that any Marine may be able to translate that information into an opportunity to affect a mission other than his or her own.

THE MISTAKE-FRIENDLY ATMOSPHERE

Though Marine officers can be hard on willful or negligent screwups, they tend to be extraordinarily tolerant of most other types of mistakes.

For starters, when a subordinate slips up, Marine officers usually look to themselves for blame. One sergeant relates how a corporal under his command forgot to process the paperwork for a training course he needed to take. "I went to my lieutenant and told him I had failed to impress on the corporal the importance of getting those papers in," he recounts.

But no matter who is seen to be at fault, failure is not the worst thing that can happen to a Marine. It's not even necessarily treated as a bad thing. True, most managers like to say they give their subordinates a certain measure of room to fail, but the Marines practice failure tolerance to a degree that would raise most managers' hair. To a certain extent, they *demand* failure: a Marine who rarely fails is a Marine who isn't pushing the envelope enough, goes the logic. Conversely, Marines who take a bold, reasoned course of action and fall on their face are likely to garner praise. "It's very hard in our society today to have this attitude," says General Steele. "With so much litigation going on, we've become a zero-tolerance society. But a commander with zero tolerance won't work for us."

PRINCIPLE #15: REWARD FAILURE

Marines see the occasional failure not only as a sign that a Marine is taking chances, as he or she should, but also as the best possible learning experience. As one captain puts it: "It's hard to keep quiet when you see someone making a mistake in training, but you have to. When that lance corporal makes the decision and sees it not work, that's how it becomes internalized."

One sergeant told me that shortly after being promoted to corporal he took a squad out on a live fire drill and decided on the spur of the moment to let a relatively inexperienced private run one of the teams. The private promptly missed a ceasefire signal, and in the few horrifying moments before the corporal realized the slip-up the private's group continued to fire while other Marines were putting down their weapons and preparing to come out from their cover. There are few mistakes that can have more serious repercussions in training; Marines are killed every year in such accidents. The corporal quickly found himself explaining to his lieutenant what had happened, even while picturing his career going down the drain. "But the lieutenant said that since no one was hurt, it was a good learning experience," he recalls. The future sergeant went to the private and told him much the same and now notes with pride that the private was eventually himself promoted to corporal.

ACT FIRST, APOLOGIZE LATER

At Hire Quality, the job placement firm that has adopted near-literal Marine practices, manager Brian Feucht describes the experience of blowing his marketing budget on a single ad without even consulting his boss, CEO Dan Caulfield. Even though the ad ultimately didn't pay off, Caulfield had a Marine-like response: "He told me he understood that I saw an opportunity and I moved to take advantage of it," says Feucht. Feucht then produces an index card, one of several given to all employees and modeled after the so-called hip-pocket cards that Marines carry around to bone up on various arcana. This particular card says, "Just do it. It's better to ask for forgiveness than ask for permission."

A notice on a nearby hallway bulletin board repeats the advice and elaborates: "We value initiative here. Do not wait to be told to do something you know needs to be done, JUST DO IT! Know the mission. Know the Commander's Intent. Accomplish the mission the best way you know how."

Needless to say, Marines won't sit by and watch while a subordinate performs an action that will cause a critical mission failure or jeopardize someone's safety. "We'll let Marines learn that way," says one colonel, "as long as the penalty isn't too great and it's not detrimental to the group."

Even when a mistake leads to real harm, though, Marines generally don't look to fry the person who made it (again, as long as the error wasn't negligent or willful). Marines recognize that they're in a dangerous business, and that truly bad things can happen without anyone being a lousy Marine. One sergeant described his experience as a head instructor at a school that taught people from all over the military how to be "inserted" from a hovering helicopter onto the ground or a rooftop by sliding down a rope. In a one-week period two students under his charge were badly injured on practice drops. Such a double disaster might be expected to bring a supervisor's career to a screeching halt. But after the school's commanders investigated the accidents, they concluded that the accidents were simply bad luck. The sergeant is now the top Marine at the U.S. embassy in Hong Kong—another fast-track position.

General Steele himself once landed on the hot seat. In 1962, when he was a captain at a Hawaii base, two men under his command and on liberty stole a boat and took it out to sea with the intention of making it to another island. The boat capsized and one man drowned. "If I had been held responsible, it would have been career-ending," he says. "But my battalion commander threw himself across the railroad tracks on my behalf." (GE's Jack Welch has said that when a manufacturing plant under his charge blew up early in his career, the supportive response of his bosses played a large role in shaping his own management style.)

In the belief that people thrive under adversity and challenge, Marine officers like to see their subordinates skirt the edge of failure. "The Marine Corps will definitely get you out of your comfort zone," explains one sergeant. But at the same time officers don't go as far as purposely pushing their people over the line into failure (except at boot camp). No matter how difficult the mission, Marines are drilled to claw out success through planning, training, information, and resources. "I set my troops up for success," says another sergeant, "so that even when everything goes wrong it's problems we've already hit and they can handle it. That takes them up to a higher level."

STARING DOWN FAILURE

On her fourth day on the job, Justice Technology's marketing coordinator, Norma Chen, was asked by her boss, marketing head Matt Jarvis, to launch a $200,000 calling-card project. "I asked him how often he wanted progress reports," she recalls. "Matt said he wanted just one, which was to let him know when it was done, and in the meantime he'd be available for questions. I said I already had a question: How should I do it? He said, 'Well, how do you *think* you should do it?' I suggested a way, and he said, 'What do you know, you answered your own question.'" The project went well, except for one glitch: Chen ordered thousands of cards printed up without an expiration date. "Matt just said, 'It's okay, just fix it, and don't ever do it again,'" she recalls. She later discovered that even though Jarvis had made it seem as if she were entirely on her own, he had seen to it that a lot of the difficult footwork had already been done by more experienced employees to ensure that she wouldn't be overwhelmed.

Remember Trilogy's OCS-like new-hire program? Throughout the three-month marathon, Trilogy CEO Joe Liemandt is said to regale the recruits with warnings that success in their final assignment is the only result that counts, and that they'll receive no credit for the effort they put into their work. But after the presentations, Liemandt reportedly tells the entire group: "I know we get up here and preach that results are all that matter... but you guys delivered a whole lot as a group."

In another seeming paradox, the Corps' tolerance of failure doesn't keep it from preaching to Marines that they should consider the idea of failing their mission an unthinkable horror. In fact the Marines join the two concepts in a simple and seamless fashion: while a Marine is in the middle of a mission or task, his or her officers will decree that failure is not an option, but if the Marine ultimately fails, the officers will usually be supportive. Says one sergeant in a motor pool: "When two broken-down trucks come in and we're told they need them back in a few hours, I tell my men we're going to get it done. But if they don't, I pat them on the back and tell them they did a goddamned great job." Another sergeant puts it this way: "If the mission doesn't get accomplished, we know it's not because we didn't put in 110 percent."

Marines are not tolerant of failure in all situations across the board. Failures in training missions, for example, are obviously regarded as far more benign than failures in actual missions. In addition, failure tolerance is adjusted downward as the level of the mission climbs. That is, the failure of a high-level mission is, as common sense would dictate, regarded with a great deal more angst than failure on a small task. As much as Marines talk about failure not being in their vocabulary, in fact they recognize that failure happens all the time in challenging environments. But when it comes to the big mission for which the Marines have been called in, failure is truly regarded as unthinkable. "Mission accomplishment is what it's all about," says Colonel Zilmer. "There may be setbacks along the way, but in the end you win." When General Krulak addresses troops, he often recounts in gut-wrenching detail the horrendous losses that Marines suffered in finally achieving a particular victory, and then leaves the group with these words: "You must not fail." Clearly Krulak is not telling his Marines that they must never fail at anything they do; he's making it clear that losing an important battle is not okay, no matter how hard you try. Marines know they have to win when it counts. (New York Republican state chairman and former Marine William Powers, asked to describe his party's philosophical position, reportedly said: "I can answer that in one word—winning.")

In the same spirit, failure tolerance also decreases with rank. Officers don't blink twice when a private not long out of boot camp screws up; it would be miraculous if he or she didn't make mistakes with some regularity. The opposite is true of generals. "A general can't look like a mortal," says Nicholas. "One failure and he's through." There's a sliding scale for the ranks in between.

As mentioned earlier, negligent or willful failures, and especially failures in integrity, are examined in a far harsher light than others. Also, as one colonel points out, the boldness that the Corps' tolerance of failure is meant to nurture is supposed to be an aggressiveness of action, not an aggressiveness of personality. "Being willing to step forward in action has to be seen as a good thing," he says. "Getting in everyone's face doesn't. People sometimes confuse the two."

Employees should get more from their managers than directions. Equally important, great managers also instill in their employees the motivation they need to apply all their skills and efforts toward carrying out those directions. In the next chapter, we look at how Marine leaders bring out levels of motivation in their people rarely encountered in other organizations.

7. MOTIVATING PEOPLE

Managers have an awful reputation within our popular culture. From movies to comic strips, the boss is an authoritarian oaf, and employees who like their work and do it well manage to do so in spite of their managers' condescension and ineptitude. These depictions resonate because we've all known bosses like this. Perhaps most aren't nearly as bad as these caricatures, but on the other hand, do a large percentage of managers actually inspire employees and make them feel valued?

Marine Corps officers and enlisted officers have to get more out of their subordinates than do managers in almost any corporation. Marines endure terrible physical working conditions, long hours, disruptions of their personal lives, mediocre pay, and risk to life and limb. And yet Marines are, as a whole, a highly motivated group willing to do all that's asked of them and more. As is true about much of the Corps, it seems paradoxical. But as is also usually true, Marines have a way of wringing logic out of the contradiction.

FINDING THE RECRUITS TO MOTIVATE

In the Marines motivation begins with the recruiting process. The Corps makes sure that process is handled by some of the most outstanding Marines in the Corps. In fact the most prestigious slots for Marines of almost any rank—the jobs that are hardest to get and that most clearly mark a Marine for a likely rise to the top—are those that involve the core personnel functions, including hiring, training, and steering the careers of other Marines. It is virtually unheard of for a

Marine to advance to a senior position without having spent at least one tour of duty of two years or so in a job that in the corporate world would be considered an undistinguished personnel position. Most successful senior Marines have performed two or three such tours.

A critical difference between Marine personnel assignments and personnel jobs in the commercial sector is that the Marine slots are temporary. Few Marines are expected to spend their entire career, or even a huge chunk of it, in a personnel job, thanks to the Corps' emphasis on cross-training. The Corps can place its very best people in these slots without having to lose them for long as candidates for mission leadership and other critical jobs. The personnel jobs, in effect, constitute a path to the Corps' top slots. Meanwhile, the Corps gets the benefit of having its hiring, training, and career-guidance functions handled by absolutely top-notch people.

PRINCIPLE #16: MAKE PERSONNEL FUNCTIONS STEPPING-STONES FOR STARS

BEING DOWN ON PERSONNEL

Personnel departments are not highly esteemed in the business world. For one thing, the function is not regarded as a fast track to upper management in the way that, say, marketing is. What's more, human resources managers tend to draw a certain amount of hostility and even disdain from employees, who typically regard them as at best uninterested in their welfare and at worst motivated to find ways to make them less costly to the company. When IBM instituted changes in its pension plan in 1999 that threatened to lower some employees' payouts, the company's HR department took the brunt of the criticism. Reportedly posted on one Web bulletin board frequented by IBM employees: "The mathematically disadvantaged half-wits in HR can't hold up a conversation on the topic of calculating anything. They are more like used-car salesmen trying to sell a car with a sawdust-filled transmission (my apologies to any used-car salesmen as you probably have more integrity than HR)."

The result of this animosity is not surprising: personnel departments don't as a rule attract a high percentage of a corporation's top performers. Put this fact together with the fact that personnel departments are responsible for much of the company's hiring practices, and it's clear that businesses have a problem.

One notable exception to the image of the clueless company HR professional is provided by American Standard, a plumbing supply and automotive component manufacturer, which sometimes asks senior executives to serve as "coaches" in roles similar to those of the Marines' monitors.

The recruiting process begins before a prospective candidate ever steps foot into a Marine recruiting office, thanks to the Corps' reputation as an elite, demanding service. Because most people know that the Corps is tougher on its recruits than the other services, it tends to attract young people who like challenges and are willing to endure those difficulties in order to be part of something special. Anyone who has paid attention to military recruitment advertising has probably noticed that while the Army, Air Force, and Navy work hard to make their service seem as inviting as possible, the Marines seem to work just as hard to make their service seem daunting.

In this way, candidates tend to be somewhat self-selecting. And of course, the better the recruits, the better the soldiers the Corps can make out of them, further reinforcing the Corps' image and leading to even better recruits—a self-perpetuating cycle. Perhaps not surprisingly, the Army, Navy, and Air Force keep falling further behind in their recruiting quotas, but the Marines continue to hit theirs year after year. In addition, the Marines have been gradually raising the standards of entry.

When prospective candidates show up at a Marine recruiting office, they aren't likely to be put off by what they see in the recruiter.

Recruiters are usually sergeants, but they can be lieutenants as well. Of the elite personnel jobs that a Marine can earn, recruiter is the most elite, and for two good reasons. First, recruiters operate with virtually no direct supervision; they have a regional boss who may be hundreds of miles away and isn't likely to drop in on them very often. Second, the recruiter is essentially selling himself or herself to promising candidates. Most candidates will have had little or no direct experience with the Corps; as far as they're concerned, their recruiter *is* the Marine Corps. Clearly it's in the Corps' interest to place its best people in these spots. Several Marines told me that they had been on their way to enlist in one of the other services when they happened to run into a Marine recruiter—and never looked back.

In addition to helping attract the best candidates, recruiters help screen out those who are unlikely to make it. This screening isn't critical, though. Hiring, in effect, is a two-stage process: poor candidates who slip through will be screened out by the rigors of boot camp. (As we've seen, commissioned officer candidates are "hired" in a similar way, but there are also some important differences in that process.)

It's easy to become too dependent on hiring. Some companies pull out all the stops to snatch up the very best people and then count on these people to shine without much support from the company. That's not the case with the Marines.

Although the Marines are justifiably proud of the job they've done with recruitment and certainly benefit from having higher-quality recruits, they don't consider it necessary to start with the very best people in order to end up with the best people. The heart of the process of turning out good Marines is not recruitment. It's what the Corps makes of its recruits that sets it apart from other organizations.

RECRUITING AND SUPPORTING

Some businesses develop self-reinforcing strengths in recruiting, as well in making the most of what they already have. When

Griffin Hospital became determined to set new standards in patient caregiving, a number of nurses and doctors chafed at the demands the policies placed on them, and many left. But the staff members who remained found the patient response so rewarding that they started going above and beyond in delivering better care. Nurses on the obstetrics ward, for example, came up on their own with a program that offers a free exam of mother and baby back at the hospital three days after discharge—or at home if a return to the hospital is inconvenient. Ninety-six percent of mothers were soon availing themselves of that exam, and in one-third of the cases a nurse identified a problem that might have otherwise gone untreated, such as jaundice or lactation difficulties. Obstetrics admissions doubled over a two-year period, and soon word got around the medical community about Griffin and its extraordinarily dedicated staff and satisfied patients. For the first time in the nearly eighty years of its history, the formerly unremarkable community hospital started getting résumés from top-notch doctors and nurses, including ones from the younger and female obstetricians often favored by expectant mothers. What's more, because the hospital's new philosophy was clearly established, the doctors and nurses who signed on tended to be those who preferred working in such a "patient-driven" model. "Our environment was becoming a recruiting tool," notes Lynn Werdal, the head of patient-care services.

After Robert Lutz left Chrysler, and just when he had agreed to take on the top job at Exide, a $2.4 billion automotive parts manufacturer that had recently announced the forced exodus of senior executives, I asked him whether he intended to bring in some of his former colleagues to give himself a clean slate of outsiders. His response: "I don't do that. I never do that. Good leaders are able to get superior performance out of the guys that are there. I learned that in the Marine Corps. You know, I've heard so many people say, 'Oh, Chrysler used to do such ugly cars, but now that you've cleaned house and gotten all these new designers, you're turning out great stuff.' Guess what? Same designers. I didn't change a single one. Insecure leaders need to surround themselves with cronies. I want to work with whatever cards I'm dealt. What a good leader does is not replace individuals, but shift that whole curve in the direction of excellence. In my eleven years at Chrysler I replaced only two people."

Or consider the fact that many companies shun young inner-city people as untrainable or unreliable. But some of the highest-performing Marines come from the inner city, and one company, CitySoft, Inc., has built a successful business employing Boston inner-city workers to build Web pages and perform other high-skill chores for clients.

GRUNTS RULE

In a visit to the Persian Gulf at the end of 1998, Defense Secretary William Cohen gave a brief pep talk to some 2,000 U.S. troops stationed there. "For the past seven years we have been able to contain Saddam Hussein," Cohen told the soldiers, who represented all the military services. The statement received applause.

Then Marine General Anthony Zinni, who commands all U.S. forces in the Mideast, gave his own little pep talk. He told the crowd that he had been asked why Saddam hadn't tried to engage the allied forces after a series of recent airstrikes on Iraq. "When I look out at you, there's no doubt in my mind why that sucker wouldn't fight," said Zinni. The crowd went wild.

It was a vintage Marine officer performance. A salient feature: in contrast to Cohen's "we," Zinni gave all the credit to "you"—"you" being primarily the enlisted men and women.

In the Marine Corps the lowest ranks are constantly told that their performance doesn't just contribute to the organization's bottom line—it *is* the bottom line. The higher the level of the officer, the quicker he or she is to deflect credit downward. Most Americans can't name a single Marine leader; even Zinni, who for many months in 1998 was probably the most important military commander on the planet, remains unfamiliar to the public. Marines who make it to the top are practically apologetic about having moved so far away from being an ordinary Marine out in the field. The single greatest concern expressed to me by the more than two dozen colonels and generals I interviewed for this book was that I was wasting time speaking with them instead of spending even more time with the privates and corporals who actually get the job done. This attitude has a tremendous impact on the self-esteem of the troops.

PRINCIPLE #17: GLORIFY THE LOWER LEVELS OF THE ORGANIZATION

The reverence in which Marine leaders hold the people way down the ladder from them is deeply ingrained and reflected in many aspects of the Corps' practices. Marines have a lower ratio of officers to enlisted than the other services, and a higher percentage of officers who began their careers as enlisted rather than entering directly into officer training. Marines are often shocked to hear what managers from other organizations think about their employees. Kirk Nicholas, the former Marine now with the Corps' Combat Development Group, tells of listening to an executive give a speech about management. "He spoke for one hour," says Nicholas, "and he never once referred to his people as 'people.' It was all 'my workers' this and 'my workers' that."

Though many executives make an effort to be seen occasionally mingling with the rank and file, few make an effort to relate to them in a meaningful way. Marine top officers shudder at the notion of not being in tune with the average Marine. "Can I get down to a Marine's level, up close and personal?" says General Bedard. "Hey, I better be able to, because he's going to be out there doing the job and putting his life on the line."

Officers at all levels work hard to break down the barriers between themselves and the enlisted. All Marines, from privates to generals, wear identical field uniforms almost all the time when on base. Rank insignia are discreet—virtually indistinguishable to the untrained eye. In training exercises instructors sometimes wear field uniforms of a slightly different hue of brown to avoid confusion. Occasionally some of the older officers wear a green, standard-issue sweater underneath their camouflage tops in colder weather, giving them the look of over-age snowboarders. Otherwise, there is nothing in their dress to distinguish a three-star commanding general from a newly minted private. The fifty-year-old general could easily look as fit as the twenty-year-old private, too. When the conditions become scorching at Lejeune, the camp raises black flags to indicate that all physically demanding activities are to be called off for health reasons. I saw a few black-flag days at Lejeune and noticed that there were still plenty of people out running—most of them looking to be Marines over the age of forty.

Even on a symbolic level the Marines are fastidious about honoring the grunt. The public is used to the image of the Marine in dress blues, wielding a ceremonial sword. Most people assume that the sword is associated with rank in some way. In fact it's awarded to privates—the only ceremonial weapon in the entire armed forces given to the lowest ranks.

I was surprised to hear one sergeant tell me that General Krulak doesn't like privates. Then he elaborated: at the end of the Gulf War Krulak summarily mass-promoted some 2,500 Marine privates first-class who had served there to lance corporal. It's not that the commandant didn't like privates; it's that he didn't like them to *remain* privates.

CONNECTING WITH THE RANK AND FILE

Business executives are quick to exhort employees to give their all for the company. But when it comes time to assign credit for the company's success, the higher the manager's level, the more credit he or she is likely to get—with the press, with the rest of the business community, and in qualitatively different levels of compensation. What's more, most CEOs and other senior managers tend to expect to be treated a bit like royalty by the rank and file.

But there are exceptions. At Ford, Executive Vice President Peter Pestillo has long been known throughout the auto industry for the respect he accords to factory workers, even going so far as to see to it that factory managers who earn the ire of workers are pushed out of their jobs. At least partly as a result, Ford's factories are more productive than those of its U.S. competitors, and the company hasn't suffered a strike in the United States since 1986; General Motors has lost billions to strikes in the past three years alone.

Lutz has little patience for executives who place themselves above the lower ranks. "You sometimes see CEOs who have big egos, which comes from insecurity," he says. "They have to be the center of attention, they intimidate people and take the upper hand right away in a discussion, and they lead by creating the kind of fear where their employees live in trepidation of their reaction. That's a terrible kind of fear. It will ruin an organization, because people become afraid of taking chances. Instead of creating destructive fear, a good leader will break down that kind of fear by talking to the troops. . . . I spent a lot of time on the shop floor and never felt that I was wasting my valuable time."

Other corners of the business world may be catching on, at least to judge from the fact that the term "servant leader" is starting to become a buzz phrase. Toro Company CEO Kendrick Melrose, for one, uses the term and reportedly advocates "turning the organization upside down, [so that] the management or leader works for the employees, and employees work for the customer."

TECHNIQUES FOR INSPIRING THE LOWER RANKS

The high regard in which Marine officers and enlisted officers hold the lower enlisted ranks, and the good relationship they generally enjoy with them, does not in any way interfere with officers' leadership responsibilities. Indeed, the relationships are crucial to the Marine style of motivating the troops.

Marine officers (I'll use the term to include enlisted officers—the corporal and sergeant ranks—for the rest of this chapter) push their subordinates' buttons, just as managers do in the corporate world. But unlike in the business world, Marines don't rely on arbitrary authority, the threat of job loss, or the promise of financial reward to get people to perform. Rather, Marines challenge and inspire their people to give their best. It's the art that Marines simply call leadership.

Motivating Marines is the most respected skill in the Corps. "You can be an efficient manager of resources in the Marine Corps and still be a leadership failure," says Colonel Barry. In fact a Marine doesn't necessarily need any other skills to be a great success as a senior officer. That may seem less surprising when applied to infantry commanders, but the Marines apply it to virtually all areas. "You don't need to know how to repair tanks to be a senior enlisted officer here. You have experts for that," says Sergeant Gentelia. "You can pick up all the specifics you need along the way. What you need to do is find ways to motivate people, to make sure that Marine doesn't feel like a wrench-turner."

This focus on leadership is why Marines hate to use the word *management*. Even though in some cases conventional management is called for—especially in logistics—it's treated as a necessary evil. "Managing is concerned with getting the maximum value for the dollar," says Brigadier General Lee, the logistics commander. "You have to do some of that in the Marines; otherwise, you could be the most beloved leader ever and you're just exhausting the organization through inefficiency. But in critical situations, you better be out there moving around in the jeep, not in your office mulling over the budget. You need to strive for a balance between management and leadership."

Major General Bedard describes how he motivates people: "I ask myself at the end of every day, 'What have I instilled in my 16,446

Marines today that will make them better and give them the maximum potential to come back alive? What more will they have to take back to society to make them that individual who stands out and who attracts others to the Marines?'"

Marine leadership works in top-down fashion: generals motivate the colonels under them, colonels motivate the captains commanding companies, and so on down the line. It may seem like bloat to have so many layers of management whose primary focus is on pushing the layer below them rather than on contributing to the bottom line, but the Marines have discovered that this is the only way to make sure that motivation fairly showers down on the lowest levels, where the bottom-line work really gets done. In this regard, Marine management structure resembles a coaching hierarchy.

There's no getting around the fact that following orders is important to Marines. When an officer hands down a formal order, there's generally no room for objecting (assuming the order is legal). Almost every enlisted Marine seems to have a weirdly fond memory of making the mistake as a buck private of trying to talk his or her way out of an order from a corporal. One sergeant recalls that when he was a private freshly arrived at his first assignment out of boot camp a corporal walked by him and ordered him to get a haircut. The private started to point out that he had just had a haircut and that his hair was regulation length, but he got no further than "But . . ." when the next thing he knew the corporal had been joined by two other nearby corporals and the three of them were all explaining to him in enthusiastic terms why it would be a big mistake for him to speak or do anything other than march straight over to the barber shop.

There's a good reason for not brooking any grief when giving an order, no matter how unreasonable or unpleasant the order may seem: in combat, when a Marine gets the order to run through a hail of gunfire to help take a position, there could be a serious problem for the squad if he feels free to question orders. "There's a time and a place for you to say, 'Do it because I said so,'" explains one sergeant. "It might be three in the morning and ten degrees, and you're trying to get a Marine out of a sleeping bag next to the one you didn't feel much like getting out of either."

But while Marines demand obedience, they don't want to rely on it. An officer whose people are constantly disgruntled about the orders they're carrying out is considered a failure as a leader and is unlikely to advance. "Obedience must be instant," says Major William Perry, "but it must also be willing. 'Willing' is more important than ever with new generations of Marines. These are Marines who think about the purpose of the job."

JUST DO IT

A *Journal of Management Studies* article reported in 1999 that almost 40 percent of decisions made by the 376 business managers surveyed were handed down to subordinates via edict. Not surprisingly, about an equal percentage of the decisions were never implemented.

Marine officers use a number of specific approaches to motivate people so that they'll carry out orders with enthusiasm.

LEADING BY ROLE MODEL

The management tool that Marines prefer over any other is simply that of being someone subordinates look up to and who setting an example that Marines are eager to follow. "Leadership means to me creating an environment of quality and of high ethical and moral behavior, and then asking for strict adherence to those standards because I apply those standards to myself," says Brigadier General Lee. "Look at this young lieutenant here. He seems to be paying attention. But he doesn't listen to what I say, he watches what I do."

Colonel Lee of OCS argues that winning the admiration of your people in one arena, no matter what it is, strengthens your ability to lead them in another. "You've got to be good at something, and then you can use that with your subordinates," he says. "I'm a good basketball player, and I play it with my captains and others whenever I can. I can learn things on the court that I'd never get anywhere else."

Colonel Barry suggests running a simple mental check on an order before issuing it. "Is it something you'd be willing to do yourself?" he says. "If not, don't ask anyone else to do it."

POSITIVE REINFORCEMENT

It's no secret that positive reinforcement of the financial ilk can bring out tremendous performances in many people. Companies like Microsoft and Amazon have built their famed employee dedication largely by awarding stock and stock options; according to the New York benefits consultancy William M. Mercer, 35 percent of 350 companies surveyed provide stock options to most employees.

But consider some of the drawbacks. People can wake up one day and realize that a big payoff isn't worth the misery of working hard day in and day out at a job they may not care much about, and for bosses they may not particularly respect. Employees can become so focused on the stock price that they take actions that drive up the stock price in the short run but do long-term damage to the company. And after slaving for years with the big payout in mind, workers can discover that the first time the company or the stock market faces a crisis and the stock craters, their payout—and their motivation—has evaporated. This isn't just speculation: Microsoft has lost dozens of its senior multimillionaire managers, including its number-two manager and the head of its office software division, to ennui or the need to find more meaningful challenges; eBay lost 18 percent of its market value in one day in 1999; and David Leach of the consultancy Compensation Resource Group in New York has said that compensation through stock options "sends a message of short term"—a sentiment that more and more experts are echoing.

Contrary to public perception, Marine officers also vastly prefer using the carrot to the stick. But they believe that the kind of positive reinforcement that works best isn't the tangible kind handed out by businesses, but rather the kind that can only come from returning to subordinates some of the admiration that you hope to earn from them. One MEU commander says: "There are always medals and awards you can give out. But what these people want is day-to-day recognition in front of their peers. It doesn't cost you anything to stroke your people in public. And it doesn't have to be anything big. It can just be, 'You did a nice job on night watch. Thank you; I noticed.'"

As Dale Carnegie noted the better part of a century ago, sincere flattery works wonders with people. Marine officers understand this principle well and rarely pass up an opportunity to throw out a little verbal ego boost. Officers routinely refer to a subordinate in their presence as anything from a "hard-charging youngster" to a "true warrior." They even have a way of calling someone "a Marine" in a way that makes it sound like the highest of compliments.

RECOGNIZING THE ABILITY TO MOTIVATE

Shaw's Supermarkets, headquartered in East Bridgewater, Massachusetts, is one company that sees at least some aspects of motivation in much the same light as do the Marines. Compensation for Shaw's managers is formally tied to evaluations of their ability to motivate and develop employees; the managers who do particularly well in this regard are fast-tracked and assigned an executive who serves as their mentor. "In a strong economy, talented people are very mobile," Shaw's Senior Vice President Ruth Bramson has said. "To retain them, you have to offer not just pay and benefits but appreciation, recognition, and the chance to grow personally in a job." It is probably not a coincidence that Shaw's has doubled in size over the past five years.

Marine officers do come down on their subordinates, of course, when they screw up. But even when dressing someone down, Marines often convey a sense of disappointment and concern rather than anger and reproach. I overheard one young sergeant questioning a corporal about the fact that the corporal had shown up for a ceremony with a wrinkled shirt. The sergeant spoke so quietly and calmly that at first the corporal didn't seem to realize that he was in trouble; he apparently thought the sergeant was genuinely curious to hear the story behind the wrinkles. The sergeant listened patiently to the convoluted explanation, which involved a confluence of a lack of closet space, missing mirrors, and non-functioning irons, and then asked the corporal to explain it again. The corporal, a little thrown off, did. The sergeant asked him to explain it a third time. This time the corporal got it. "There's no excuse for these wrinkles," the corporal said, standing up a little straighter.

"That's right," said the sergeant gently. "There isn't. And this isn't the sort of role model that you want to bring back to your men to look up to, is it?"

The corporal, who was roughly the size and shape of a bookcase, seemed to shrink under the sergeant's steady and slightly saddened gaze and shifted his body in different directions as if the oxygen had run out in his location and he was searching for a fresh pocket. Without raising his voice, or even looking or sounding angry, the sergeant had probably not only ensured that the corporal would never appear in miscreased shirts again but also that the corporal would walk away with a lesson in facing up to errors that he would tell his grandchildren about.

As another sergeant put it: "When I'm disciplining a Marine, I'm not angry at him, I'm disappointed that I've failed to make him understand. I want him to see that I care, and he's let me down. It's not to put him down, but to pull him up."

Needless to say, Marine officers do occasionally reprimand their subordinates in more conventional, angrier terms. That's perfectly acceptable now and then, insists one colonel. "But you have to take a look at yourself if you're using the hammer too often," he says.

CARING

Marine officers find ways to communicate the idea that they aren't merely interested in getting the best possible performance out of their people, but that they genuinely care about their welfare. Again and again in conversations with Marine officers, the notion came up that their primary responsibility is to see to it that the people under them thrive and end up safe and sound. They don't think in terms of sacrificing performance and mission success in order to accomplish these paternal goals but rather believe the two are ultimately interdependent. "Whatever your goals are in the Marine Corps," says one colonel, "if you aren't taking care of your people, you won't achieve them."

General Bedard says that the change-of-command ceremonies for his subordinates that he presides over offer him a chance to reinforce this all-important notion. "During the ceremony," he says, "I tell the new commander, 'Look around you, and understand that you're responsible for everything that happens to each one of these Marines. And remember that everything that happens to each Marine carries over to thousands of people: his wife and kids, his brothers and sisters, his parents, his friends, his whole hometown.'"

Most Marines even believe (correctly, for the most part) that their boot camp DIs were sincerely concerned for their welfare, despite the hair-raisingly harsh figures they cut at the time. Kirk Nicholas describes his DI: "He had taken a grenade years before, and the two halves of his face didn't quite line up," he says. "When he got angry at you, only one half of his face would get red, and spit would fly out." At the time it was a frightening sight, he concedes, but now he looks back fondly on that DI as a caring individual.

Nicholas also tells of a sergeant he knows who had recently noticed that one of her subordinates was acting agitated. When the man didn't show up for work and didn't answer his phone one morning, she decided to drive out to his apartment to check on him. She found him sitting on a chair holding a gun, which she was able to talk him into giving to her. There aren't many private-sector employees who could count on that sort of intervention.

PROMISES, PROMISES

There are plenty of caring business executives. But it's interesting to note that some of the businesses that have developed the strongest reputations for generosity to employees have had to renege on their implied commitments when things became tight, creating tremendous discontinuities in the corporate culture and disaffection among employees. IBM, for most of its history an extremely paternalistic organization, went through a wrenching series of downsizings in the 1980s that decimated morale. Even cozy cultures like that of the ice-cream manufacturer Ben & Jerry's have been strained by an era of tighter competition. Peoplesoft, a Silicon Valley software success story famous for an employee-friendly environment that included promises of lifetime employment and generous benefits, stunned its workforce with layoffs after a dip in growth in 1999. Japan's entire commercial sector has been struggling with its inability to support the long-standing Japanese tradition of ironclad job security.

The caring on the part of Marine officers is genuine, but it also provides a payoff. Says a colonel: "The men can see which officers are worried about their own performance instead of worrying about the people working for them. If you work for the Marines who are under you, in the end they make you look better."

Though Marine leaders take care of their people, they don't coddle them, and they don't make unrealistic promises. They give a lot, and they demand a lot. In the long run, this attitude keeps Marines at all levels more satisfied.

Challenge

Most Marines wouldn't be in the Corps if they didn't enjoy challenges. Officers recognize this fact and understand that part of their job is to make sure that no matter what job a Marine has, he or she regularly gets to feel the excitement of facing a test of his or her competence and character. That doesn't simply mean burying them in work—though most Marines do in fact carry impressive, if not frightening, workloads. It means linking the workload to a meaningful achievement, whether it's a competition, the chance to contribute to a critical mission, or an opportunity to learn an entirely new skill.

One way officers challenge Marines is by getting them to think of their opposition in the most daunting possible terms. It's a no-lose proposition: if the opponent really does prove to be that tough, then the Marines are prepared; if the opponent proves to be easy pickings, then the Marines can celebrate a smashing victory. Colonel Zilmer recalls describing the Iraqi threat to the Marines preparing to invade Kuwait during the Gulf War. "We built the Iraqis up as a much more capable force than they were," he says. "No one had any doubt that we'd beat them, but it's better to underestimate our own capabilities than to underestimate theirs."

DISSING THE COMPETITION

Boeing managers have been sniping for decades at their rival Airbus Industrie in Europe, claiming it's an inefficient company propped up by government subsidies. Meanwhile, Airbus has been busy cutting the manufacturing costs of its components by up to 44 percent and slashing delivery time in half to nine months—as Boeing's costs have mushroomed and once-loyal customers have defected. In a similar vein, Netscape managers famously sneered at America Online as a second-rate service right up until the day AOL acquired their company.

INVITING OUTSPOKENNESS

Marines seem as a rule to be somewhat laid-back when they're not accomplishing a task—perhaps because they face enough exhausting challenges to feel they ought to relax when they get the chance. Or maybe ease flows from the self-confidence with which the Corps imbues them.

In any case, whatever mellowness Marines exhibit at times, it does not extend to keeping their mouths shut when they think the wrong thing is being done. Officers demand that their legal orders be unhesitatingly followed, but they don't expect their people to refrain from questioning their style, their analysis of a situation, their decisions (before they become orders), or their opinions. In fact they encourage and in some cases even require subordinates to speak up loudly and clearly about such matters. One of the quickest ways an officer can short-circuit his or her career is to ignore or squelch a Marine of any rank who is airing concerns. Knowing that their opinions are valued and dissent welcomed by their bosses and by the Corps in general frees Marines from building up resentment of authority, a sure sapper of motivation.

PRINCIPLE #18: DEMAND TO BE QUESTIONED

Colonel Moore, the MEU commander, recounts the time when a lowly second lieutenant pointed out during an exercise planning session that the plan Moore had approved would subject a covert landing party to a high risk of discovery. Moore acknowledged the concern but overruled him; what Moore couldn't explain was that as one of the people who had devised the exercise, he knew for a fact that the landing party wouldn't be discovered at that point and that if the landing party came in a different way it would foul up the exercise. The second lieutenant objected again, and Moore again overruled him, but more brusquely. After holding his tongue for a while, the second lieutenant objected yet a third time—and Moore suddenly realized that the young man was right. "I had been 'fairy-dusting' the exercise," Moore says. "I was using information I wouldn't have had in the real world to make decisions. I was wrong, and here was a second lieutenant calling a full-bird colonel on it in front of the entire group." Moore let the landing party use a different approach, even though it threw off part of the exercise.

In fact Marines can be heard speaking their minds in almost any setting. Though it is illegal for a member of the active military to be openly "contemptuous" of the president, one Marine major nevertheless published a letter in the widely read *Navy Times* calling President Clinton "an adulterous liar" with regard to his behavior in the Monica Lewinsky scandal. (The major was officially told to knock it off, but his action was widely cheered by Marines.) Few people familiar with Marines were surprised to discover that Scott Ritter, the defiant head of the United Nations' arms inspection group in Iraq who violated virtually every unwritten rule of diplomacy in facing down anyone who tried to interfere with his group's mission, is a former Marine.

The *Marine Corps Gazette* provides, among other things, a forum for the airing of debates, complaints, and criticisms. Most Marine officers read the publication carefully, looking for any sign that the Corps may be ignoring a better way to do things.

THE *EXIDE GAZETTE*?

"One thing lacking in businesses is a way to allow employees to give feedback openly," says Lutz. "There's no equivalent to the *Marine Corps Gazette*. . . . Not only is that a way to find out where you might be screwing up, but it's a great way to identify future leaders." He adds that at Chrysler he relied on anonymous surveys of his subordinates to gauge his own performance—and that he's been considering starting up some sort of internal publication at Exide that would be analogous to the *Gazette*.

Marines get criticism from the outside, too, of course. They can take it, but they're not required to take it quietly if they think it's unreasonable. Consider this exchange, which ran in the *San Diego Union-Tribune*:

February 4, 1999

Is Harassment of Residents the Role of the Military?

My quiet neighborhood of Del Mar Terrace near Torrey Pines Reserve is a haven for families, retirees, single people, young couples—a variety of citizens who share appreciation for nature and peaceful, quiet living. On January 27, there was an invasion of our beach and coastal area. More than one hundred flights to and from the ocean, and up and down the coast, took place on this one day alone. There were easily fifty helicopters in the air—the noise was deafening. It was a strange, almost science-fiction war scene enacted by Marines in the sky.

This area is our home. It's a residential corridor, not a battle zone. We are not at war. Is the invading enemy the very military force that has protected and served our nation over the years?

What is the role of the military in our country? Certainly not the harassment of our residential neighborhoods and disturbance of our scenic view corridors.

Helicopters have no right to take over the skies of residential North County. Is this Apocalypse Now, San Diego?

Maura Harvey
Del Mar

February 8, 1999

Re: "Is Harassment of Residents the Role of the Military?" ("Letters," February 4)

Responding to Maura Harvey's letter wondering if the Marine helicopter training flights that passed above her Del Mar home were simply to harass residents, I can say that, yes, our mission is to harass residents, specifically Mrs. Harvey.

We do not train twenty-four hours a day, seven days a week, to provide freedom and security to all residents of the United States. We exist only to annoy the very people we are sworn to protect, against all enemies, foreign and domestic. We spend months and years overseas, away from our families and loved ones, in some cases making less than minimum wage, choosing to live a life in which many qualify for food stamps, just to have the chance, one day, to annoy people like Mrs. Harvey.

There is no more sought-after position in the military than the Maura Harvey Annoyance Task Force. As a matter of fact, the Marines who spent Christmas dug into fighting positions in northern Kuwait and their brothers in the sky, braving antiaircraft missiles and artillery, were just training to come back to the States and fly missions over Mrs. Harvey's house.

It has nothing to do with the security of the nation. It has no impact on our ability to carry out missions in Africa, the Middle East, and Eastern Europe, and it has no bearing on Mrs. Harvey's ability to enjoy "nature and peaceful, quiet living." The "strange, almost science-fiction war scene" she described was put on solely to make noise and to destroy her "scenic view corridors" in Del Mar Terrace. It certainly was not valuable and necessary training to help sustain the lives of those who ensure this nation's freedom should they ever be sent into harm's way to do just that.

Next time, Mrs. Harvey may want to look upon those loud machines and think about the men and women who fly, ride in, and maintain them. Ponder the sacrifices they make in providing this nation with the warm blanket of freedom we all enjoy. Maybe she might even imagine how much more disturbing it would be if she were not sure what country the helicopters were from, or whether they were going to attack her beautiful neighborhood.

But she shouldn't worry too much about that, because we will not let it happen.

Capt. John F. Peterson
USMC Pacific Beach

LISTENING

Marine managers make a point of listening carefully to what their people are saying, whether it's critical or not. "I've never seen a good commander who didn't listen really well to what's percolating," says Colonel Beavers. "The guys who are good leaders take it in. They aren't always thinking about their comeback while someone else is talking."

One high-ranking sergeant who meets regularly with generals and colonels says he rarely attends a meeting where a junior officer doesn't pipe up. "The senior officer always makes a point of staying quiet and of not correcting him," says the sergeant.

Brigadier General Lee notes that an open-door policy is inefficient and exposes a commander to trivial gripes. But he maintains one anyway. "When you shut the door on someone with a minor point to make," he says, "you risk having them not come back the next time when they have something to say that's good for the organization. Even if I see what they're doing as whining, they don't see it that way, and if I help them figure out how to deal with it, they probably won't need to come back unless it's for something important. When you do that, there's been a passing on of power."

The passing on of power and motivation to Marines is just one facet of a broader change in those who join the Corps. We've touched on this transformation at least implicitly throughout this and the preceding chapters, and now we focus on it in the next one.

☆ ☆ ☆ ☆ ☆

8. CULTURE

Never underestimate the power of a group of people who believe nothing
can keep them from success and who are willing to do anything to achieve it.
—T-shirt in a Quantico shop

Captain Kenneth Humphrey is trained in "radio recon," one of the most admired and hard-to-get jobs in the Marines. Only sixty people are trained in this black art, and they are given an extraordinarily difficult, dangerous, and critical mission: crawling close enough to the enemy to observe its actions firsthand and then transmitting the information back to the Marines. Humphrey not only has received Marine training to this end but has also been sent by the Corps to train with the rest of the military's toughest and most elite combat units, including the Navy SEALs and the Army's Rangers and Special Forces. In any other branch of the military, Humphrey's fatigues would be festooned with the various coveted patches and pins representing this extraordinary level of skill and fortitude. But there isn't a molecule of fabric or metal on him that differentiates him from any other Marine. Indeed, nothing about Humphrey—in his demeanor, in his daily job, in the way other Marines treat him—suggests that there is anything special about his place in the Corps.

According to Humphrey, one of the SEALs with whom he trained, and with whom he became good friends, tried to convince him to join the SEALs. As a SEAL, the friend pointed out, he would get to skip the grunt work and focus on the more glamorous missions. He'd get to play with the highest-tech toys on the planet rather than the more mundane equipment on which the Marines tend to rely. Instead of being one of the crowd, he'd get the full star treatment that the Navy confers on the SEALs. Humphrey had to mull it over for only a second. "It all sounded great," he explains. "But I just couldn't get past the idea of being called 'sailor' instead of 'Marine.'"

If there is any one aspect of the Marine Corps that can be given special credit for its stunning effectiveness, it is the culture of pride, dedication to the group, and hard-driving confidence that is deeply ingrained in almost all Marines. Though the Corps has many strengths, most of them build off of this one. Indeed, the real value of many of the Marines' practices lies not in the direct gains they offer but in the role they play in establishing and reinforcing the culture.

An organization can get a lot of things wrong and still succeed brilliantly if it manages to instill and maintain a culture as strong as the Marine Corps culture.

PRIMARY VALUES

Though the Marine culture, like any true organizational culture, is seamless and somewhat amorphous, it can be deconstructed into key elements—that is, a set of shared values. In the Marine Corps these values work together to support the Marines' capability-based organizational mission.

PRINCIPLE #19: INSTILL VALUES THAT SUPPORT THE MISSION

Marines have codified what they refer to as their "core values" of honor, courage, and commitment. Though these attributes are certainly cornerstones of the Marine character, the different (if overlapping) set of six primary values I describe in this chapter may be more relevant to other organizations.

1. COMMITMENT

The Corps helps Marines develop and nurture strong individual identities, but they also learn to let a large part of themselves transcend those identities. As a result, the typical Marine finds that the line between who he or she is and who the Marines are is not entirely clear.

The Marine motto is, of course, the Latin phrase *semper fidelis*, or "always faithful." This motto, which might be uttered, heard, and read a hundred times or more in a Marine's typical day (usually condensed to *semper fi*), is as noteworthy for what it does not attempt to convey as for what it does. It does not explicitly exhort Marines to do a great job, protect the country, be brave, or exalt the organization. It simply demands that every Marine remain committed to the Corps and to other Marines, unconditionally and forever.

Clearly the Marine Corps is asking a bit more of its members than do other organizations. In companies where it's every person for himself or herself and the only sure way to obtain commitment is through stock options, it would simply seem ludicrous to ask for unqualified lifetime loyalty. That's too bad, insists Major General Bedard. "The best way to measure an organization is by the loyalty it inspires, bottom line," he says.

Even among the military services, Marine solidarity is legendary, even if it is sometimes perceived as a little over the top. For instance, Army troops at the fierce Ranger infantry school in Fort Benning, Georgia, eventually become used to seeing every Marine in sight drop to the ground each time a single student Marine is ordered by a DI to do push-ups.

The loyalty isn't limited to a Marine's term of service. Marines bristle at the phrase "ex-Marine," claiming there is no such thing; there are only "former Marines." Senator John Chaffee of Rhode Island, a former Marine, has pointed out that when he talks with veterans of the other services in the halls of Congress about their time in the military, they talk about who they *were*, but when he talks with former Marines about being in the Corps, they talk about who they *are*. Guest books at the visitors' barracks on Marine bases are usually filled with effusive comments from retired Marines of all ranks and their spouses who have made a happy vacation out of a return visit to what looks for all the world to the rest of us like a hellish training grounds. After the Oklahoma City bombing, when the effort to recover bodies was called off pending the stabilization of the debris, word got around that a Marine guard was among the out-of-reach fatalities. Within minutes former Marines started stepping out of the crowd of rescue workers and into the shifting rubble. Before long the group was carrying out the body of their fellow Marine.

Marines speak of the Corps with unabashed pride and affection. For those of us grown used to workplace cynicism, it can be jarring to hear a Marine refer to his or her "beloved" Corps, or simply to "loving the Marines." I examined faces and voices for hints of irony the first few times I heard terms like these, or at least for signs that they were rote phrases repeated out of habit, but I never detected any.

Of course, when you have an organization full of people who love the institution and are more than happy to talk it up, you get a lot of good PR—one reason the Corps is so highly regarded by the public. The other military services, like many businesses, are often wary of the press and cagey about what they say to the public, but the Marines seem eager to tell anyone just about anything about the Corps, short of giving away classified information. The resulting good press feeds back into the Marines' sense of pride.

ABSOLUTELY, POSITIVELY COMMITTED

Federal Express CEO and former Marine Fred Smith has managed to instill a high level of commitment throughout his company, supported by, among other things, a policy of developing managers within the rank and file and giving generous benefits to even part-time workers. When the pilots' union—the only union that has managed to establish a foothold at the company—threatened to strike in 1999, thousands of employees swarmed into the streets of Memphis to show noisy support for the company; even many pilots urged the union to call off the planned shutdown. The union settled. Meanwhile, a pilots' strike earlier in the year at Northwest Airlines and a teamsters' strike at FedEx's competitor United Parcel Service the year before wreaked havoc with those companies.

2. INTERDEPENDENCE

During the Vietnam War, when a Marine squad of ten or so men suffered casualties, other Marines were quickly pulled in to bring the squad back to full strength. That, says Captain McBreen, proved to be a mistake. Now Marine policy is to allow a squad that has suffered losses to remain as is; if the squad ultimately takes heavy losses, then the entire squad is rotated out of action. The reason: the sense of teamwork is so strong on a Marine squad that adding new people—no matter how good they are—tends to reduce its effectiveness. "It's better to stay with the same knucklehead a long time than it is to have a bunch of different sharp guys coming in and out," says McBreen.

Most of us struggle to find a way to stand out in our jobs. Marines, too, want to stand out; they are as driven as any human beings on the planet to excel. But far more important to most Marines is succeeding as part of a team. To some extent, the Marines' nearly fanatical devotion to teamwork is related to their devotion to the Corps as a whole. Being loyal to a unit—be it a battalion, a platoon, or a three-man fire team—is one way to convert the more abstract loyalty to the Corps into an actionable sentiment. But in other ways it's different. An employee may feel a bond to the company without being particularly interested in helping out the other people in his or her department; indeed, backstabbing is a way of life in some organizations. But the Marine value of interdependence makes it crystal clear: Marines are both dependent on, and devoted to helping, the other Marines with whom they work.

This interdependence—Marine taking care of Marine—comes up in all aspects of Corps practices. Unlike the other military services, and many businesses, the Corps frowns on referring to its people as "assets," with the term's vague implication that people can be regarded in the same light as equipment or information or money—as tools to be used by decision-makers. Instead, Marine units are referred to in terms of "support." Every Marine job, from fighter pilot to mechanic to clerk, is defined as a means to support other Marines.

Part of the emphasis on teamwork is about winning: Marines are taught from the moment they enter the Corps that the isolated, individual effort ultimately leads to failure and that teamwork equates with success. But Marine teamwork is also about taking care of one another. Once a Marine makes the commitment to do virtually anything to protect a fellow Marine, he or she also comes to the realization that the same will be done for him or her, and the two notions become self-reinforcing.

Every Marine has a story about being helped by comrades. Some tell of starting to fall behind on long training marches from injury or exhaustion and being carried for miles by squadmates. One sergeant told me about the time a truck slipped its parking brake and pinned him against another truck. Rather than risk wasting time searching for the keys, six Marines pressed their shoulders against the front of the runaway five-ton vehicle and somehow managed to push it a few feet back up the slight incline, freeing the sergeant. Many Marines insist there is no combat mission more motivating than one intended to rescue a Marine pilot shot down behind enemy lines. And as with loyalty to the Corps, the habit of taking care of fellow Marines doesn't end with active service. When former Marine Manuel Babbitt was sentenced to be executed for murder in 1999, more than 600 Marines who had fought alongside Babbitt three decades earlier in Vietnam wrote letters pleading (ultimately in vain) for a commutation on the grounds that he had been suffering from post-traumatic stress syndrome.

As one young Marine explained to me, Marine interdependence has nothing to do with Marines having to *like* one another. "We don't all get along," he says. "But we all help each other."

3. SACRIFICE

At the Marine Corps' 223rd Birthday Ball—Marines commemorate the date of their founding as a birthday rather than an anniversary, preferring to treat the Corps as if it were a living thing—General Krulak stepped up to center stage to address the celebrants. An observer unfamiliar with the Marines might have expected the normally upbeat and charismatic general to mark the happy occasion with various bon mots and congratulations. Instead, Krulak delivered a multimedia presentation graphically detailing the carnage that the Marines suffered in taking the island of Iwo Jima in World War II.

It's not as if the Marines don't have plenty of less tragedy-laden victories to point to. For example, the taking of the island of Tinian, which was fiercely defended by the Japanese in World War II, is widely regarded as a model of successful amphibious warfare because the Marines took the island with the lowest ratio of Marine-to-enemy casualties of the war. But Marines hardly ever bring up Tinian outside the classroom. Instead, they constantly evoke the tragedies of their most costly battles: Iwo Jima, Okinawa, Tarawa, and others. Indeed, it's hard to have a conversation with a Marine without encountering some reference to Marines dying. The walls of Marine office hallways are often lined with combat photographs of Marine wounded.

In other environments the fixation on casualties would seem morbid and even defeatist. In the context of Marine values, such references are ennobling and inspiring. Marines have made embracing the need for sacrifice a deeply rooted and highly positive part of their culture.

Marines come to associate sacrifice with personal, professional, and organizational excellence and learn to take pride in it. It's not a shallow stoicism; no one asks Marines to not be afraid, or to not complain. As Marines like to put it: "A Marine who isn't complaining isn't alive."

When Marines talk about those who have fallen in battle, they are honoring them, and a portion of that honor reflects on themselves. It reinforces Marines' sense of being part of something special. That's why Marines love to boast about putting up with worse conditions than their counterparts. The comment of one retired Marine officer is typical: "In Vietnam we ate nothing but C-rations for two and a half months, while the Army was getting two hot meals flown in every day."

The exalting of sacrifice can also be seen in the pride that Marines take in doing more with less. The Corps is intensely frugal as an organization, and Marines frequently claim that having fewer nonpersonnel resources pays off in several ways. For one thing, it reinforces the notion that the Marines are about people, not things. For another, Marines believe that working on the relative cheap makes them a good deal in the eyes of the public, which hears constant bickering between Congress and the other armed forces over the latter's pleas for more spending on aircraft, ships, and weapons systems. "We like America to see what they're getting for their money in the Marine Corps," as one colonel puts it.

Having to get by with fewer resources also inspires innovation, claim many Marines. "We've never been sufficiently resourced to accomplish the jobs we accomplish," brags Brigadier General Lee. "When we were in Saudi Arabia, I told my troops it was a good thing. Everyone always wants more Marines and more equipment, but if we got it then we'd start counting on it to solve our problems instead of trying to think of new ways to do things."

Some Marines say, for example, that the Corps' emphasis on achieving high combat impact by concentrating strikes from fast-maneuvering, small groups arose in part from a lack of enough troops to fight in conventional style. "The Army can afford to spread everything out," says one officer.

PRIDELESS SACRIFICE

All businesses ask their employees for some measure of sacrifice. At young Silicon Valley companies it's not unusual for executives, programmers, and marketing managers to work sixteen-hour days; sometimes they even sleep at their cubicle before picking up again the next morning. Along the way these employees often lose their family, their personal life, and in some cases their emotional balance—several Silicon Valley psychologists specialize in treating overworked managers. Workers all over America accept job-related miseries, from frequent transfers in location to customer abuse to physical hazards on the assembly line.

Why do people put up with it? In Silicon Valley, on Wall Street, and in executive suites the relentless work is largely a chase for stock options, salaries, and bonuses. Others overwork themselves or suffer through poor working conditions because the job demands it and they can't find a better one. Rarely are the sacrifices associated with commitment and self-respect.

In the same vein, corporate frugality generally is not regarded as a point of pride or as an inspiration for innovation; rather, the saved cash is seen as an end in its own right. Other businesses, meanwhile, believe that lavish spending on compensation, facilities, and perks is virtually a requirement for building and maintaining a leading-edge company. It's interesting to note that some venture capital firms are said to eliminate businesses from investment consideration simply on the basis of their fancy digs. Marines would approve of the practice. Dan Caulfield of Hire Quality certainly does: his offices are located in a Chicago neighborhood as gritty as any Marine base town, porno shops and all, and visitors are treated to the sight of cracked plaster, leaking steampipes, and worn, mismatched carpeting.

4. PERSEVERANCE

Marines have banished the word *retreat* from their vocabulary, preferring to use terms such as "rearward action." This is partly because the Marines' fast-maneuvering style often does indeed require that they temporarily move backward as part of an offensive. But it's also because even when Marines have to back off from the enemy because they are being overwhelmed, they refuse to think of it in any terms that smack of giving up. "You never hear the word *defeat*," says one enlisted Marine. "We learn to just keep pushing, pushing, pushing."

The World War II island battles provided stunning proof of the Marines' determination to keep charging, no matter how grim the situation, until they finally gained the victory. General Krulak noted at the Birthday Ball, when speaking of Iwo Jima, that one Marine mired in the gruesome battle later said he never doubted that the Marines would take the island; he only wondered whether it might be the last Marine left alive who claimed the victory. (The celebrated photograph of the squad of Marines planting the American flag at Iwo Jima did not mark the end of the battle; the fight was still raging at that point, and it continued for a few more days. The flag-planting was intended as a statement of confidence and determination—the combat equivalent of Babe Ruth pointing into the stands.) The message to Marines is a simple one: you can't fail if you don't stop trying.

It's worth mentioning again that Marines distinguish between the failure of an entire Marine force in the overall battle and the failure of a part of a force in a smaller action or even of a single Marine in his or her task: the former is regarded as unthinkable, but the latter is understood to be occasionally inevitable (and as we've discussed, even desirable). It's also important to recognize that the Marines regard a must-win attitude, along with other elements of what Marines refer to as spirit or character, as more essential to a Marine's ability to contribute to victory than talent, skills, or physical strength. "A lot of Medal of Honor guys are five-foot-six and weigh 140 pounds," says one colonel. "You can't measure spirit in physical stature."

5. CONFIDENCE

Groucho Marx famously said that he wouldn't want to belong to any club that would accept him as a member. The Marines build on the converse of this sentiment: if an elite and demanding club accepts you as a member, then you must be something special. That is, Marines derive confidence and self-esteem just from being a Marine. Built into the Corps' practices are constant reminders that the Marine organization is an elite one—and thus, by extension, that individual Marines are among the elite.

But the Marines don't let it rest with that. As we've already seen, the Corps has found ways of turning almost every event in a Marine's life, large or small, into a confidence-building exercise. The way Marines train, the way they receive orders or feedback—everything is designed to make them feel good about themselves and their ability to get the toughest jobs done, even as these same practices challenge them and force them to stretch. And of course, confidence and success are self-reinforcing. "We develop the true ingrained spirit of believing we're the best," says Major General Bedard. "And then we perform to that."

The idea that confidence plays a large role in success also supports the Marines' emphasis on leveraging their strengths rather than trying to win through brute force. As Gangle puts it: "War is a simple mind game. You don't have to kill the enemy to defeat him. You only have to convince him that you can defeat him. The first step to doing that is to inculcate the idea in your own people that they are better than anyone else." (For what it's worth, a study published in 1999 in the psychology journal *Child Development* found that the most reliable predictor of a student's academic success was how confident the student was in succeeding—regardless of his or her academic skills and previous level of success.)

Marines don't confuse confidence with cockiness. If the former is regarded as essential to success, the latter, as discussed later, is seen as a potentially fatal flaw.

6. BELIEF IN MISSION

As odd as it may seem, the Marines frequently and openly praise many Nazi management and military practices, in conversation and in classrooms. They're comfortable doing so because they are perfectly clear about what made the Nazis so despicable and believe that the Nazis' twisted ethics ultimately negated their considerable strengths. One major, speaking to a few hundred young captains, asked, "Did the Nazis have values? Sure. They were intelligent, talented, and focused. They had very effective leadership. But they weren't in line with the right principles."

Although many Marines have strong religious values, a more generic view of morality seems to be universal among them—one that holds sacred dignity and basic human rights. When the Marines take on a mission, they want to know they are on their way to upholding these principles somewhere in the world. Or more simply put, the Marines draw much of their strength and motivation from their conviction that they are the good guys. "We have to come back to the belief that what we do is a noble mission," says Zilmer. (The occasional business leader feels much the same way. Gregory Slayton, CEO of MySoftware, a Silicon Valley firm that saw its stock price nearly quintuple in 1998, has said: "You have to get your people excited about their role in the big picture—to give [their work] something of a noble purpose and show that it's for the betterment of society.")

The Marines tend to be particularly clearheaded when it comes to recognizing, analyzing, and in some cases borrowing from their opponents' strengths. It doesn't feel threatening or disloyal to the Marines to do so because they're secure in the belief that their opponents *deserve* to lose. True warfighting excellence, according to the Marines, requires passionate belief in what the organization stands for, not simply a desire to dominate others, exact revenge, or win territory.

DOMINATION FOR ITS OWN SAKE

It's interesting to note that despite Microsoft's phenomenal performance over the past decade, a growing number of observers have come to predict that the company will face tougher times. The reason often cited: Microsoft has simply made too many enemies and has come to be seen by some as a vaguely evil enterprise, owing to its apparent obsession with dominating as many markets as possible. In the 1970s IBM also came to be viewed as a greedy company that simply couldn't strong-arm enough competitors into oblivion to satisfy itself; the company crashed in the 1980s.

The Marines are the first to admit that they themselves have on occasion lost their grounding in the principles on which they've built a sense of rightness of mission. The My Lai massacre, in which an Army unit slaughtered some 500 helpless residents of a Vietnamese village, including women and children, is a frequent talking point in Marine discussions, serving as a springboard for examinations of Marine atrocities during the Vietnam War. Their reflections on these experiences have helped Marines come to terms with their role in the loss of the Vietnam War and contributed to their confidence that they won't make the same mistake again.

As one general puts it: "An amoral approach to profession carries grave repercussions."

It is to a large extent the Marines' belief in the importance of a cause that makes them so effective in humanitarian missions. Not only does the Corps throw itself into these assignments with surprising motivation for a group of warriors, but it frequently goes well beyond the given mission. Gangle recounts asking for volunteers among a Marine force at port in Bangladesh to unload 100-pound sacks of rice from a relief boat in stifling heat and humidity; more than 2,000 Marines stepped forward every day. Bedard recalls the 130-man rifle company that offered to give up a liberty weekend— precious time off for Marines stationed on a ship—to lay tile at a Kiwanis park in Halifax. In Somalia, he adds, Marines coming back in the morning from an exhausting all-night patrol would often stay up another few hours to teach English classes for local villagers. In

Sierra Leone a Marine colonel directing the evacuation of Americans ignored the State Department rules limiting the evacuation to U.S. citizens and sent a team into an active combat zone to airlift to safety the children in an orphanage; three hours later the structure was demolished by a shell fired by local forces. Describing the incident, a Marine adds, "That's why we're Marines." This sense that they are doing good in the world is a strong driver behind many of the Marines' success-producing traits.

7. INTEGRITY

Much of the world was stunned in 1999 when the Corps did not convict two Marine aviators for flying low enough in their F-16 to slice through a cable on a crowded ski-resort gondola in Aviano, Italy, the year before, causing more than a score of civilians to plunge to their death. Equally baffling to many was that the Corps then turned around and convicted the two men for destroying a cockpit video of the flight. The two judgments seemed all out of proportion.

But from the point of view of the Marines, the rulings made perfect sense. The cable-cutting incident was the result of the sort of warrior-culture rule-bending that the Marines tend to tolerate. Though horrified over the civilian deaths, the Marines accepted the fact that in the dangerous environment of realistic training, and with the risk-taking mindset the Corps encourages, things are sometimes bound to go wrong and havoc can result. (One civilian was killed and four injured in yet another Marine training mishap in Puerto Rico in 1999.) When it happens, Marines don't look for scapegoats among their members; they take the heat as an organization for their practices. But destroying the cockpit videotapes and then initially lying about it—that was a betrayal of Marine values that could never be tolerated.

The Corps would frown on any Marine who claimed to embody flawlessly all of its values. But if every Marine is expected to fall a bit short in one area or another now and then, the one type of slip for which there is almost no tolerance is unethical behavior. Again and again Marines of all ranks emphasized to me that they could put up with almost anything else in a fellow Marine. The Corps recognizes more than most other organizations that we live in a world of growing complexity and ambiguity, but when it comes to integrity there is, as one officer puts it, "a razor-sharp line." While the military at large has been plagued in recent years by a series of scandals involving unethical behavior, ranging from sexual harassment to procurement kickbacks, the Marines have remained relatively free of such charges. "What Marines do is trust each other," says one general, adding that this trust is essential for operating in a high-speed, complex operation built around interdependence. When the trust is shattered by a lie or other ethical transgression, Marines tend to bring down the hammer on their own.

Needless to say, not all Marines and former Marines are paragons of virtue. It was reported that Jeffrey Papows, the CEO of IBM's Lotus Software division, frequently regaled colleagues and customers about his colorful career as a "backseater" in Marine jets when in fact he had, according to the Corps, a brief and uneventful stay in the Marines as an air-traffic controller. Papows may not have made it very far in the Corps, and such indiscretions may be relatively rare, but Marines find this sort of transgression by a former Marine infuriating and disturbing.

SECONDARY VALUES

There are other values instilled by the Corps that, if not as essential to Marine effectiveness as the primary values, still play at least a supporting role.

Boldness: The Corps doesn't want to build swaggering, fearless people hell-bent on committing acts of reckless heroism. But it does want its people to be bold—that is, to take initiative and, when in doubt, to act rather than mull things over while critical events are unfolding.

Adventurousness: One thing that Marines hate to see is a Marine going through the motions. They even have a special phrase for it: "going admin." Marines look for excitement from their work. As one Marine puts it: "There is some juice in knowing that tomorrow you could be landing on a ridge forcing a dictator to back down; it's electric." Another quotes a colleague: "To be a good Marine you have to be mature. But every good Marine also has a little boy in him." (Of course, many executives would be thrilled just to have more of their employees reach the level of "going admin"—that is, getting the minimum requirements of the job done.)

Humility: Despite the emphasis the Corps places on confidence, and in stark contrast to the popular image of Marines as almost arrogant, the Corps actually cultivates humility both on a personal and an organizational level. And for a good reason: a lack of humility tends to lead to underestimating the enemy and disregarding one's own limitations. Marines expect to win, but they don't expect to win by allowing themselves to end up grossly outmanned and outgunned, or even worse, by being outplanned and outmaneuvered. Marines receive the message that they are expected to pursue perfection but must never allow themselves to believe they've achieved it. Their opponents' capabilities (if not their motives) are treated with respect, and Marines learn to expect their own plans and efforts to go awry.

Frankness: Marines aren't expected to hold their tongue when they think a mistake is being made or a process needs fixing. Indeed, they're exhorted to speak out when they have a thoughtful criticism to make, even if it means confronting a superior officer.

Professionalism: Marines do nothing in a sloppy, halfhearted, disreputable, or negligent way. Not everyone in the world is happy to see the Marines land, but few people repeat the mistake of not respecting them. One sergeant recalls that in Haiti the Marines were nicknamed "whitesleeves" because their sleeves, when rolled up, showed a lighter color than those of the Army soldiers. Word quickly got around the population that the whitesleeves were not to be messed with. "The Army guys were constantly having their covers [hats] and water stolen," says the sergeant. "Us, never."

EMBRACING PARADOX

Robert Lutz likes to quote F. Scott Fitzgerald's assertion that the test of a first-rate intelligence is the ability to hold two opposing ideas in the mind at the same time and retain the ability to function. The importance of cultivating seemingly contradictory traits is a lesson he learned in the Marines, he says, and it became important to the way he ran Chrysler.

Almost every value and characteristic that can be identified in the Marine culture is balanced by one that in some way opposes it. It is often in this balance, rather than in the individual traits, that the Marines' values achieve their full power. Dealing with complex environments calls for a nonsimplistic, non-extreme mindset, and the tension between traits can provide the needed subtlety and variation in outlook.

PRINCIPLE #20: CULTIVATE OPPOSING TRAITS

We've already alluded to a few of these tensions: confidence versus humility, for example, which allows Marines to envision success without underestimating the enemy; being individualistic versus identifying with the organization, which enables Marines to find their own style for contributing to the team; and being loyal to the organization versus being encouraged to criticize it, which allows Marines to support the Corps while finding ways to improve it. Here are some others, most of which have either already been addressed or will be elaborated on later:

- A need to risk failure versus a need to succeed
- Being empowered versus respecting the hierarchy
- Having well-defined plans and processes versus needing to improvise
- Being disciplined versus being creative
- Having a core job versus handling different functions
- Carefully analyzing versus acting quickly
- Having to compete against other Marines versus having to place their success above your own

Organizationally the Corps itself is in some ways a paradox, embodying both the seasoned execution of careful plans and processes and a free-flowing, seat-of-the-pants opportunism. Or to look at it another way, the Corps combines the best of a large, successful industrial corporation and a hot Internet start-up.

PRIMING THE CULTURE: BOOT CAMP

Boot camp tends to get too much credit for the Marine Corps culture. Without question, the twelve-week transformation of an aimless nineteen-year-old who has never faced a serious challenge and has little self-respect into a confident, highly disciplined, intensely motivated soldier prepared to give his life for the Corps and his fellow Marine is a nearly miraculous one. The problem is that the whirlwind physical and emotional trauma (and ultimate triumph) of boot camp is designed to provide a shock entry into Marine culture—and shocks, while effective in the short term, don't in themselves necessarily make for a lasting change. Indeed, even Marines and other observers who praise boot camp's transformational powers concede that its effects can start to dissolve within a year. The ultimate success of the Corps in inculcating culture depends more on the everyday environments in which Marines spend their time.

Still, there are certain boot camp philosophies that can provide organizations with useful insight into how to jump-start the process of inculcating culture. Actual Marine boot camp practices based on these philosophies are probably of little use to the business world, but there's no reason why the basic approaches can't be applied in less extreme forms.

MAKE HIRING CONDITIONAL

As with OCS, a person arriving at boot camp has not been accepted as a Marine. As a recruit, he or she must make it through boot camp, with all its stress and tests, before becoming a member of the Corps. The harder a thing is to obtain, however, the more highly it is regarded: besides serving to eliminate those who would be unable to meet the Marines' standards, the rigors of boot camp ensure that those who make it through will be all the more proud to join.

CREATE A HIGH LEVEL OF STRESS

Boot camp is physically and emotionally brutal. Recruits are kept hungry, exhausted, sleep-deprived, disoriented, and intimidated. In this state their resistance to change is broken down and they're more amenable to accepting new points of view if doing so helps them make it through the ordeal.

LET FAILURE LOOM LARGE

In the initial weeks recruits are set up to fail over and over again in almost everything they do. Hanging over them, meanwhile, is the fear that they will fail in the largest sense—by not being accepted into the Marines.

CORRELATE SUCCESS WITH TEAMWORK

Further along into boot camp, the recruits learn that they can start to rack up some small victories if they worry less about their own performance and more about how their platoon as a whole is doing. This is where recruits start to understand the roles of sacrifice, interdependence, and perseverance. One slightly crude example: during bathroom breaks seventy men are sometimes given two minutes to use five stalls. If the teamwork isn't strong, the results are unpleasant.

Explicitly State the Cultural Values

Drill instructors and officers at boot camp find any excuse they can to elucidate the Corps' values and the ways in which these values will help the recruits succeed. Hearing this advice from people who have obviously excelled in the Corps, at a point when the recruits seem so helplessly immersed in failure, can have a powerful impact.

Supply a Big Success

At the end of boot camp recruits run the Crucible, a hellish obstacle course that just weeks earlier would have seemed utterly impossible. But the vast majority of those recruits who have made it this far will succeed; the Corps wants them to come away with the lesson that they can accomplish the seemingly impossible if they cleave to the right values. As one colonel puts it: "To do more than they think is physically and emotionally possible is a self-release. As long as they're willing to keep trying and don't let their spirit get broken, they'll succeed. And they'll come away with the spirit of succeeding at any cost."

There's one more philosophy applied in boot camp, one that's so central to the Marine culture that it's worth highlighting as one of the main management principles.

Principle #21: Establish a Core Identity

Boot camp recruits become proficient in riflery and hear a hundred times that "every Marine is a rifleman." They will hear it thousands more times throughout their stint in the Marines. Three-star generals and privates alike quote it at the slightest excuse. (Though OCS recruits don't spend as much time on riflery as those in boot camp, the concept is further pounded home to new officers in The Basic School.)

On a superficial level, the statement simply refers to the fact that any Marine of any rank in any job anywhere in the world might be expected at some point to pick up a rifle to support fellow Marines and protect people and property in a firefight. In that sense, the core identity is a shared experience and excellence, on top of which other skills are built. Cooks know how to set up a perimeter defense, and aviators can hold their own in a ground firefight. In Somalia, Marine transport specialists driving food and supplies from the port inland were often called on to defend the trucks against raiders.

But more important, the core identity of rifleman refers to a bond among Marines that cuts across rank and specialty. It's a way of stating that all Marines have the same job, no matter what form that job takes, and that in the end everyone in the Corps is working toward a common goal: to make sure that the infantryman on the ground is successful. If you're not the soldier shooting the bullets, then what you're doing is in some way supporting the soldier who is, and that's what makes your job valuable. The core identity keeps everyone's eye on the same ball and encourages mutual and self-respect.

ORGANIZATIONAL EMPATHY

As an example of how a company can establish a core identity, consider Griffin Hospital, where the staff is constantly bestowing unexpected acts of kindness on patients. "I ran into someone from our environmental [housekeeping] staff today wheeling a patient down the hall," says Vice President Lynn Werdal. "She had seen him sitting there, so she just left her work, took over, and brought him to where he needed to go. Every employee of

this hospital is considered a caregiver, whether they're process-
ing bills in accounting or cleaning labs." Even the parking lot
guard considers himself a caregiver, going out of his way to
escort patients into the hospital or help absentminded visitors
find their cars. Because there are no signs inside the hospital
pointing out the way to different wards, visitors and patients
must ask a staffperson for help. When they do, that person
won't simply point the way—indeed, staff pointing in the hallway is banned at the hospital—but will personally bring the
inquirer to his or her destination.

Griffin also illustrates how a company can utilize a high-
stress environment to nurture desired values. Every few months
twenty-four employees at a time—a mix of nurses, doctors,
administrators, technicians, housekeeping staff, and other personnel—are taken to a monastery hidden away on Long Island.
At this tranquil but spartan facility the employees take turns
playing the roles of patients who are afflicted in various ways:
blind, bedridden, wheelchair-bound, paralyzed, and so forth.
Experiencing the resulting sense of helplessness makes the participants more aware of what the hospitals' patients are going
through and also promotes bonding among the hospital staff,
every single one of whom eventually goes through the process.

AFTER BOOT CAMP:
THE PERMANENT TRANSFORMATION

The intense Marine culture gets its start in boot camp but is fully
developed and maintained by a pervasive and complex web of practices, traditions, and interactions to which Marines are constantly
exposed throughout their careers. It happens through a simple for-
mula: the Corps' leaders—men and women in whom the culture has
been deeply instilled—do everything they can to transmit the culture
to everyone under them, including those who will someday become

the Corps' new leaders. In this way the culture becomes self-reinforcing and self-perpetuating. The Corps' values are not simply force-fed to Marines like Dilbertian management edicts. (Time Warner tried pushing some 1,000 executives through a two-day values seminar in 1999, but the effort reportedly met with mostly skepticism.) Marines learn the values by being exposed to people who live them. Almost everything a Marine says or does seems to have a values-related message as a subtext.

Marines never pass up an opportunity to boost a younger Marine's confidence. "If you tell a guy enough times that he's the best," says one colonel, "eventually he'll start to believe it. That makes a person very dangerous to his enemies. People with that attitude are not beatable." If confidence flags in the face of a series of daunting obstacles, Marines are told to try this trick: instead of thinking about beginning at the starting point and then having to defeat each obstacle along the way to the finish, think about being at the finish, having already conquered all the obstacles; then envision in reverse order the path that led to this success.

You hear the resulting pride, confidence, and enthusiasm in the Marines' language, typified by the odd noise, similar to a walrus bark, that Marines constantly employ. It is apparently never inappropriate to make this barking sound; with the right inflection, it can be utilized in informal conversation, full-dress ceremonies (yelled out randomly from the audience), briefing sessions, and hard training. You also see it in the Marine walk, particularly that of corporals and sergeants. It's almost a strut, slightly formal while at the same time relaxed and jaunty. "I tell my youngsters," says General Bedard, "even in street clothes and long hair, people should never have trouble recognizing you as a Marine."

One of the most powerful weapons Marines employ in transmitting the Corps values is the vast store of Marine Corps tradition. Marines' knowledge of their own combat history tends to be exhaustive, and they rarely pass up an opportunity to throw out a historical reference. The message: twenty or so generations of Marines have through their sweat and blood handed you one of the world's great legacies of excellence, and now you've become its caretaker. "An organization can use its history to establish a foundation of pride," says Colonel Barry, "providing an incentive to match it or even do better." Or as one sergeant puts it: "We're here *because* of our tradition."

In addition to being exposed to a sense of overall Marine Corps tradition, young Marines are also constantly subjected to sea stories, which could be thought of as personal traditions. We've looked at how sea stories are used to teach problem-solving skills. They're also crucial transmitters of values. Starting in boot camp, Marines hear—and eventually share—a never-ending stream of tales of Marines who managed to pull off a difficult task, screwed up in a surprising way, or simply ran into something they'd never encountered before. The nominal topic of a sea story is often trivial and sometimes even tawdry, and the emphasis may seem to be more on entertainment value than on education. But in fact a subtle set of themes run through most of these stories: Marines do what it takes, Marines take care of one another, Marines uphold the honor of the Corps, Marines share a common mission. Every modestly experienced Marine has at least a few choice sea stories about events in his or her own career as well as a trove of stories gleaned from others.

LEVERAGING A YOUNG TRADITION

There aren't many companies that can point to a history and set of traditions as deep and rich as those of the Marines. On the other hand, some companies do pretty nicely with what they've got. Justice Technology employees love to show off the company's beat-up former headquarters, now its warehouse, complete with dents from the countless basketball games played there during some of the long workdays that stretched into the small hours of the morning. When Justice's tsunamic growth mandated a new headquarters, the company bought a fancier building in Culver City in the Los Angeles area and promptly gutted and remodeled it to look something like a colorful, ultramodern version of . . . its old warehouse.

CEO David Glickman has in general worked mightily to establish and maintain a counterculture culture that plays off the free-wheeling early days of the company. The company offers free dog care, will subsidize anyone who skateboards to work, and treats the entire company to lunch the day before payday. There are plenty of sea stories, many of them describing pranks that trumpet the company's skill at applying technology in surprising ways. One favorite story is that of a group of managers hiding high-powered speakers in the ceiling of one employee's exceptionally junk-strewn office and rigging his computer so that the arrival of e-mail was announced by an ear-splitting, ultra-high-fidelity performance of the theme from *Sanford and Son*.

At trade shows, when competitors showed up in spiffy matching golf shirts and hats, Justice's people marched in sporting matching mechanics' jumpsuits. If the sun and waves are right, second-in-command Leon Richter and Matt Jarvis, the marketing head, take their first meeting of the day on surfboards. And Glickman recently added a two-story phone to the front of the building. "It will be the world's largest working phone," he beams. "There'll be a small booth at the bottom where anyone can make a free call to anywhere in the world."

The Corps further strengthens the bond between Marines and the organization by providing many of the attributes of a family. Marines often speak of the Corps as loving, nurturing, accepting, and forgiving. Gunny Willie Bennett, who has the build of an aerobically fit ox, is a thirty-seven-year-old man with seventeen years in the Corps. After his first four undistinguished years, Bennett found himself in front of a disciplinary board that gave him a week to answer a simple question: Did he want in or out? With the help of various mentors, Bennett turned his career around and is now assistant director of one of the Corps' leading enlisted officers' schools. "The Corps put so much pride in my body, it's hard to explain what it feels like," he says.

Once a part of that family, a Marine has to screw up very badly, or else with great frequency, to convince the Corps that he or she doesn't deserve to stay a part of it. "When I see a discharge come across my desk," says one general, "I try to look into that Marine's heart and see if there isn't a little light showing through. Is there any way we can give him another chance? Imagine the inner turmoil it causes in a young person who's made the transformation into a Marine and then has to turn away from it."

The Corps makes a great effort to blur the lines between the sort of family experience it offers Marines and each Marine's actual family. Marine officers and enlisted officers learn that they can't understand their subordinates unless they know something about their subordinates' spouses and children or, in the case of younger Marines, their parents, siblings, and even grandparents. One young sergeant visited a nonmilitary friend at his workplace while on leave and was shocked by what he found. "I met a manager there who didn't know the names of all his employees," he says, shaking his head. "Here you know the names of everyone in your people's families. I'm a single parent myself, and I appreciate that my boss knows that, and he understands that sometimes I have to go home to be with my daughter when she's sick."

DRAWBACKS TO THE CULTURE

Is the Marine culture intense enough to be called cultlike? It probably depends on how loosely we want to define "cult," but in any case the question doesn't seem worth quibbling over. If the culture causes Marines to exhibit remarkable fealty to a cause and to make stunning sacrifices for it, at least most of us would agree that the cause is a good one. Some of today's most successful companies have also been accused of being cultlike, including Microsoft and Amazon. Colonel Barry doesn't even mind comparisons between the Corps and inner-city street gangs. "Gangs provide their members with a sense of identity, with father figures, with leadership, with the opportunity for promotion, and members will lay down their lives for it," he says. "The Marine Corps is a gang alternative."

Some observers have suggested that the Marines, in their devotion, discipline, and enthusiasm, are drifting away from the mainstream of society and becoming resentful and antagonistic. They were famously called "extremists" by one administration official (who quickly became an ex-official), and it has even been implied that the gulf between the Marines and the rest of society could eventually widen to the point where the Marines might be tempted to lead a coup. All I can say to this is that after having spoken at length with scores of experienced Marines, few of whom seemed the least bit reluctant to say exactly what was on their minds, I didn't encounter a single one who expressed undue hostility toward society at large. To me, Marines seem acutely aware of the ways in which they stand out from society, but this sense of separation seems to take the form of pride in excelling rather than alienation. If some Marines are critical of society or government, the feelings and their expression seem well within normal bounds, at least after taking into account that Marines are trained to be outspoken and bluntly honest. This bluntness sometimes makes Marines seem less tolerant than the rest of us, who may harbor the same sentiments but have been taught to be diplomatic about how we express them.

One exception: the Marines as a whole seemed far more furious than the average citizen with President Clinton's affair with an intern and his subsequent disingenuous testimony about it. This angry disgust makes sense in light of the Marines' feelings about integrity, and the fact that they hold the president, as commander in chief, accountable to their ethics and values. Even so, the Marines seemed perfectly satisfied to express their disgust for the president through sensible channels.

Even the Corps itself has not always lived up to the standards set by its own culture. Many officers and senior enlisted officers speak openly of the Corps' problems in maintaining discipline, pride, and excellence in the 1950s and again in the 1970s. But Commandants Alfred Gray and Charles Krulak are widely credited with restoring the Corps over recent years to its full potential—or at least as close to its potential as Marines will allow themselves to admit to getting.

The appropriateness of an organization's culture—and of all its attributes—must ultimately be measured in terms of mission success. In the next chapter, we return to an examination of Marine hands-on, bottom-line practices and view the tactical umbrella under which the Marines pull together their various competencies in planning and executing a full-scale confrontation.

☆ ☆ ☆ ☆ ☆

9. TACTICS

I'll tell you everything you need to know about tactics—
hit the other guy as hard as you can when he's not looking.
—Anonymous sergeant to private in an oft-told sea story

Daylight breaks over the weed- and scrub-speckled hills, casting sharp-edged and intricate shadows over the desert floor and leaving a pattern that closely resembles the camouflage paint job on the Hummers briskly and bumpily snaking their way in convoy along an unpaved road. The beauty of the natural scenery is eerie, but eerier still are some of the man-made sights we pass with increasing frequency as we move deeper into the desert: hulks of tanks pockmarked with holes in some spots and charred in others; slapdash plywood constructions the size of cottages but with no obvious function, or the smashed remains of the same; large stacks of old tires leaning wildly or altogether collapsed; and craters, some as big as good-sized swimming pools, which occasionally encroach onto the road itself, necessitating some last-moment swerving by the drivers.

We are at 29 Palms, a Marine facility that takes up 932 square miles of the Mojave Desert in California. Eight of these square miles contain roads, buildings, and other trappings of more or less ordinary civilization. The rest (within certain environmental constraints) have been set aside as terrain on which the Marines can utilize every sort of aircraft, land vehicle, and weapon of destruction in their formidable arsenal. All military services have practice grounds, but two things distinguish 29 Palms from its counterparts elsewhere. First, all of the various types of combat arms are practiced at the same time, in the form of large-scale maneuvers meant to simulate precisely the highly integrated, complex, fast-moving conflicts in which the Marines specialize. Second, all the bombing, shelling, and shooting involves real bombs, shells, and bullets, often within surprisingly close range of some of the thousands of Marines taking part in the exercise.

Today's mission: a Marine infantry battalion, supported by air, tank, artillery, logistics, and other groups, is to defend a rocky patch of the desert. Though the enemy is imaginary, this sort of large-scale, live-fire exercise provides one of the ultimate tests, outside of genuine conflict, of the Marines' abilities. It will not only call on every aspect of their training but also require them to apply all of these aspects simultaneously and in close coordination. If these Marines haven't yet mastered tactics, it will quickly become apparent in the coming hours.

The context in which Marines apply tactical thinking typically bears little similarity to those in which most organizations operate. But the principles by which they develop their tactical plans are in fact quite broadly applicable, and for good reason: the Marines need them to work not only in the vast range of combat situations they've already identified but also in situations they haven't conceived of yet. These principles don't specify particular tactics but provide a framework, a set of sensibilities that guide tactical decision-making in complex, fast-changing, intensely contested arenas.

(What Marines term "tactics" is what many organizations would loosely call "strategies." Marines are generally strict, however, about reserving the latter term for planning that takes place above the level of combat—the decision-making, often by political leaders, that determines the goals of a war, or even whether a war should be fought at all. Decisions about the plans and actions needed to win battles fall under the rubric of tactical or in some cases "operational" thinking.)

Today's 29 Palms exercise also presents an opportunity to see the Marines apply not only their principles on tactics but their principles related to command, distributing authority, nurturing talent, and other areas. What's more, the simulated battle will demonstrate just how quickly and persistently things can go wrong in an intensely competitive environment.

PREPARATION

The 29 Palms exercises, like real missions, are focused not on a standard battalion of Marines but rather on a MAGTF assembled from different battalions. Most of the units in this exercise have been drawn from Camp Lejeune and placed under the command of Colonel Walt Davis. Davis plays against type for a Marine battle commander: slim and slightly stooped, he normally speaks in a relaxed Jimmy Stewart drawl. This morning, though, Davis is a little hoarse and edgy. He has been working long hours trying to get the kinks out of the battle plans. He didn't get to bed until close to midnight last night, and then he showed up at four o'clock this morning to work out some last-minute details.

Also up late last night and early this morning was Colonel Michael O'Neal, the commander of the "Coyotes," the nickname of the Marine unit that oversees the exercises at 29 Palms. The term is used with great respect among Marines. The Coyotes, wearing uniforms the color of desert soil, were handpicked for this assignment and are highly skilled in the complexities and dangers of integrated, live-fire exercises. They are responsible for both the safety and the success of the Marines who come here to train. In wartime the Coyotes are often shipped out to beef up other units, as was the case during the Gulf War. O'Neal, a more typically hale-and-hearty style of commander, eyeglasses aside, headed up the lead tank battalion during that war and is renowned for his tactical expertise. Despite the tough pace at which he's been operating for the past week, and the fact that he bicycled several miles through drizzle to hook up with the convoy before dawn, O'Neal looks relaxed, refreshed, and eager to get going.

Today is not the MAGTF's first shot at this mission, nor will it be their last. In classic Marine style, the 29 Palms exercise is designed to let the participants suffer through a certain amount of failure in facing what seems an insurmountable challenge, and then work their way up to overcoming it. Earlier in the week the Marines worked on the offensive portion of the mission. Today the MAGTF will carry out the defensive portion in the desert. In two days the entire mission, offense and defense, will be run nonstop. By then Davis and his Marines will be expected to shine. Today falling short will still be regarded as a step toward ultimate success.

Nevertheless, Davis doesn't want to have to take advantage of that margin for error. For one thing, mistakes today could carry tragic consequences: four of the last eight exercises here involving a Lejeune MAGTF have resulted in the death of at least one Marine. Most people killed or injured here are victims of vehicle accidents—typically someone driving a Hummer in a nighttime maneuver and wearing night-vision goggles, which reduce depth perception, ends up driving off a ledge. In fact one of Davis's Marines did exactly that two days ago, though fortunately he escaped with only moderate injuries. But Marines also sometimes fall victim to their comrades' bullets here.

Why use live fire? The Army, for example, runs large-scale maneuvers similar to these, but with laser-based fire simulation gear. There are two problems with simulations that lack live fire, notes O'Neal. First, live fire can be psychologically devastating to those unused to it. "Nothing can take the place of the heat and dust and confusion of real fire," says O'Neal. Being exposed to it all here lessens the shock of real combat. In addition, an absence of real danger fosters what the Marines call "John Wayne" behavior—a willingness to take extra risks because, after all, the price for failure is having your laser-detection vest beep and then sitting on the sidelines. This behavior, once learned, can have tragic consequences on a real battlefield.

BAD RISKS

In recent years several instances have been made public—and probably dozens more kept quiet—of young managers taking it on themselves to engage in extensive and highly risky financial trading on behalf of their apparently unknowing employers, ultimately losing many millions of dollars. It may be that top managers at these firms failed to impress on their less experienced colleagues the very real, and very unpleasant, consequences of any form of John Wayne behavior.

The drawback to a live-fire exercise is that there can't be live people playing the role of the enemy, for obvious reasons. Instead, the Coyotes keep convincing track of the positions, actions, and losses of an imaginary enemy force and provide plenty of inorganic targets for the Marines to pulverize and riddle with holes. Actually, by avoiding a face-off between Marine units, this arrangement carries a distinct advantage: no one has to lose. In contrast, the Army runs a famed "Red" unit that specializes in standing in for enemy forces in exercises. Because of its repeated training in these maneuvers, the Red unit often wins. From the Army's point of view, the lessons learned in going up against and sometimes losing to an elite "enemy" unit are invaluable. From the Corps' point of view, allowing a large group of Marines to leave an exercise on a note of failure is anathema.

If Davis's group does fail, it won't be because it hasn't been given a healthy assortment of Marines and assets. At Davis's beck and call will be an infantry battalion, an air group that includes F-18s, Harrier "jump-jets," and Cobras, an artillery battalion, a tank battalion, two platoons of amphibious assault vehicles, and a combat engineering platoon ("combat engineering" being a more formal term for "obstacle reduction," which is itself a euphemism for blowing up anything that stands in the way of advancing Marines). It is the tight combination of such a range of people and resources, the Marines insist, that allows them to leverage the actions of a relatively small MAGTF into a devastating force.

That, and a plan that makes use of good tactics. Davis hopes he has one. But he also knows that however carefully the plan is drawn up, there is a good chance it will go out the window when the first shot is fired. As Zilmer points out: "The Gulf War happened exactly as we planned it. That was an aberration."

THE PLAN

Major Michael LeSavage, Davis's executive officer, provides an overview for the other officers during a final briefing. "The enemy's strength will be speed and momentum," he says. "Its weakness will be the terrain."

Marines don't look for a fair, head-to-head fight; they try to put the fix in. That means coming up with tactical plans for a battle in which they can draw on their strengths while robbing the enemy of the opportunity to draw on its own.

PRINCIPLE #22: MATCH STRENGTH TO WEAKNESS

One key enemy weakness: unlike the Marines, most foreign armies tend to fight under centralized command, using predictable tactics. Davis and his team have a pretty good idea of what the attack will look like when it comes. There will probably be three waves: the first will be an armored reconnaissance patrol that will try to spot an open avenue of attack; then an advance guard will try to pierce the Marines' defenses; and finally a main guard will pour into whatever opening the advance guard has cut out.

The MAGTF leaders recognize from having been on the offensive side so many times that the attacker controls the clock—it determines when the attack will occur, and how quickly. (One example from the business world: when the leading online brokerage firm E-Trade suffered service outages in 1999, its more traditional rivals chose that moment to launch ads pushing the reliability of their services.) To compensate, the defender has to take advantage of its ownership of the territory by trying to force the attacker to confront it on ground where the defender has an advantage. (Microsoft has mastered this defense: by incorporating into its immensely popular

Windows operating system new software programs intended to counter a competitive thrust into another segment of the industry, the company is in effect forcing its competitors to take on Windows.)

It may be impossible to stop the attacker from advancing, but the defender can pick away at the attacker as it advances and steer it into a trap. To do this today, the Marines are going to try to funnel the enemy's main force into a canyon, seal it in, and then pound it. In this way the enemy's speed and momentum will, it is hoped, carry it to its destruction.

Most important, everything that the Marines do has to come as a surprise to the enemy. When it comes to combat tactics, surprise is the Marines' overriding consideration.

PRINCIPLE #23: SURPRISE AND DISORIENT THE OPPOSITION

Marines make no bones of the fact that in any battle they like to get the first blow in, and the less the enemy is prepared for it the better. This isn't to say that the Corps wants to instigate armed conflicts. But when the mission makes combat inevitable, they want to be the ones to kick it off.

Colonel Barry relates an incident that took place when the Marines were in Haiti in 1994. Some of the Haitian policemen were providing hostile resistance to the Marines, and in one firefight between Marines and the police ten policemen were shot. When word got out to the press, reporters crowded around the Marine regimental commander, Tom Jones, and one reporter asked him whether the rumor that the Marines had fired on the police first was true. "I hope so," said Jones to the nonplussed journalists.

Marines want to leave the enemy as disoriented as possible. To do so, they not only strike first but also try repeatedly to hit the enemy at times, in places, and in ways that the enemy is least likely to have anticipated. As part of this effort, the Marines try to work some form of deception into every major mission. During the Gulf War, according to Zilmer, the Marines sent a small force arranged to look like the tip of a larger one speeding into Kuwait, drawing the Iraqi's artillery fire. The fire allowed the allied forces to pin down the location of the enemy artillery units and destroy them. Meanwhile, the Marines' main force was speeding into Kuwait along an entirely different path. "We set the Iraqis up so that they felt they couldn't rely on their own senses," says Zilmer.

The focus on leveraging attacks to have maximum psychological impact is a critical one for the Marines, and it's one of the hearts of maneuver warfare. A demoralized opponent is unlikely to fight well, no matter what its advantages.

MANEUVER COMMERCE

Some businesses have made good use of a surprise-and-disorient style. When PepsiCo introduced a clear cola called "Crystal Pepsi," Coca-Cola quickly launched "Tab Clear"—and backed it with an intentionally ineffective marketing campaign. The company wanted to create confusion in the marketplace that would kill the product category and protect sales of its best-selling traditional cola.

Or consider Frontier Airlines, a tiny carrier that has gone head to head with United Airlines in United's main hub city of Denver and elsewhere. Major airlines ferociously defend against incursions into their hubs, and the list of small airlines that have been chased out of these cities is a long one. But Frontier has employed sneaky tactics to tie United's hands. Among them: the company waited until United had fixed its summer schedule in its computer systems before suddenly announcing that it was adding Denver flights so that United would have had to reprogram all its systems to react; rather than setting up several flights a day on a few routes, as is standard practice for smaller airlines, Frontier scheduled only two flights a day on several routes so that United would have to spend a fortune to respond on all the routes; and Frontier scheduled its flights as far apart as possible from United's connecting flights, so that any flights United added to compete at those times wouldn't offer convenient connecting flights and thus would be relatively unprofitable. As a result of all these tactics, Frontier's traffic climbed 35 percent between mid-1998 and mid-1999.

OPENING MOVES

Before a single shot is fired, two things have gone wrong for the MAGTF this morning.

First, a key operations officer from Davis's group has been sent home because of an illness in his family, and his absence will leave a less seasoned officer in his position. Though this switch will leave the team at less than peak form, it's not seen as detracting from the exercise. To the contrary, Marines regard the sudden loss of key personnel as normal to the course of war, and they want to train for it.

The second problem involves the four "scout snipers" sent out the night before by the MAGTF. The snipers have done their job a little too well: they've managed to find a hidden spot close to a key attack location along the expected enemy route—so close that the Marines won't be able to shell the enemy at that location as they had planned because of the risk of the snipers being hit by a slightly stray shell.

Davis orders the battle kicked off, and Marine artillery starts pounding on the enemy's air defense and fixed artillery units, which have been identified by "national assets"—one of a wide range of euphemisms employed by the military for "satellites," about which most information is classified.

Artillery is a surprisingly complex science and art. The Marines who operate artillery batteries attend the longest Marine training school outside of aviators' school. The 150mm Howitzer on which the Marines rely looks like a small industrial smokestack set on wheels and is capable of hurling 100-pound shells a distance of about 12 miles at the rate of 4 per minute. It also fires rocket-assisted shells that can be shot 27 miles and reach heights of as much as 36,000 feet—well into the air space of the commercial jets that fly over the Mojave. (Needless to say, the Marines don't put this capability to the test at 29 Palms.) When the Howitzer is fired, the force of the discharge blast rattles the internal organs of anyone standing within 30 yards or so of the gun. A series of delicate calculations are required to ensure that all this power ends up destroying the right things—calculations that take into account everything from the density of the upper atmosphere and the temperature of the big gun's barrel to the earth's rotation under the speeding shell. Yet with all this precision, the Howitzer fire team, when pressed, relies on the same trick learned by Marines on the rifle range, a trick called "Kentucky windage": when a shot falls to one side of the target, simply aim at a spot equally far away on the opposite side of the target. Marines aren't afraid to take shortcuts when speed is critical.

One of the key decisions that must be made about a multiple-Howitzer artillery barrage is whether to execute it as a "series" (the guns keep firing one after another) or as "groups" (all the guns fire at once). A series is generally more physically destructive because all the guns can keep firing at will and can more easily adjust their fire to correct for inaccuracies. But groups have advantages, too. When the opening round of a series hits, the enemy tends to be completely unprotected. By the time the second round lands, 60 percent of the enemy on average is under cover. So Marines know to make the opening shot count and thus prefer to start off with a group. Equally important, Marines often favor groups because of the psychological effect of a barrage hitting all at once. Indeed, Marines prize artillery for the psychological toll it takes as much as for physical devastation it causes.

GROUP THERAPY

The advertising community has long understood the concept of groups versus series. Ad executives, for example, know that a company with a limited budget will make a bigger impression by grouping its ads—that is, buying a short but intense barrage of media exposure rather than spreading its ads thin over a longer period of time. On a more abstract level, any intense action taken by a company that captures a lot of attention in the marketplace without a sustained effort or a relatively large investment could be regarded as a form of grouping. One example is Chrysler's Viper, the ultra-high-performance sports car developed at unprecedented speed—three years from concept to production—and at relatively low cost. Though the Viper was introduced with much fanfare, it never received a full-fledged, long-term marketing campaign—and yet it came to symbolize the resurgence of Chrysler's entire product line in the early 1990s.

The twenty-five or so Coyotes scattered around the MAGTF offer virtually no help during the exercise other than to provide the MAGTF with information about the imaginary enemy that it would normally be able to observe on its own. (For a little extra realism, they discreetly toss what are essentially shrapnel-less grenades near Marines who are "under attack" from the enemy. To liven things up even more, they also occasionally put shoe polish on artillery sighting eyepieces and pass out crackers with live tarantulas on them.) But they keep a close eye on the artillery, requiring that every single coordinate be run by them before a shell is fired. O'Neal himself has set up a small observation post on a tall hill in his Hummer, where he sits listening to traffic on three different radios and plots all the artillery shots and troop movements on a map on his lap. He seems to be able to visualize the trajectory of every shot fired, occasionally muttering about shots that he can see are going to end up off-target. But these don't concern him as long as they're not heading toward any Marines. The Coyotes' motto: "Safe and stupid, let it go; smart and dangerous, shut it down."

DIRECTING THE BATTLE

Once the battle begins, Marines like to keep things as fluid and unrestrained as possible. But there are certain rules of thumb that they rarely violate.

Stay hands-off

Colonel Davis and his MAGTF command team have set up headquarters in a large tent. Inside it's gloomy and cramped, with nearly a dozen officers huddled over maps laid out on tables, manning radios and scribbling notes. Davis himself is sitting in a chair near the back of the tent. Every so often he blurts out a question: Has the unit tried mortars? Have they tried a different radio network? But for the most part he looks like someone who's out of the loop.

He's not, of course, but in classic Marine style he's leaving as much of the decision-making as possible to the people below, and especially to the commanders on the front lines. Indeed, Davis made it explicit in his statement of commander's intent that things should run with minimal involvement from him. Besides, most of the MAGTF command team's work is already behind it. The team heads up the overall planning, but carrying out the plans and—more important—changing the plans on the fly is mostly left to the commanders of the individual battalions and other units. Only if a potential conflict arises between units does MAGTF command get involved.

Davis admits to being more hands-on than many MAGTF commanders. Some of them, he says, make a point of staying away from the command tent out of concern that even their silent presence is a distraction. Zilmer puts it this way: "The trick is to be in a place where you can command, but not where you have to control and coordinate."

But Davis stays in the tent because he likes to listen to radio traffic, from which he says he gets an intuitive sense of how things are going. The radios are chattering almost nonstop because the command tent acts as clearinghouse for information for the force. At first it sounds as if the Marines have become bogged down in chaos.

The locations of two Cobras are unknown, as are those of three infantry platoons, because of mix-ups about which of the several dozen radio networks various units are supposed to be using. But Davis shrugs it off. "First reports are never as good or as bad as what's really happening," he says.

Get a Firsthand View

Soon, says Davis, he'll drive out to a high piece of ground over-looking the heart of the battle. No matter how much information he has available at his fingertips, he explains, nothing can take the place of seeing the battle firsthand and gathering "ground truth." As the U.S. military has become more and more high-tech, top command has gained the ability to run remote-control wars. But one sure way to stunt a career in the Marines is to become perceived as a long-distance commander. "Most of the time a regimental commander has to stay a little farther back, to get a broader view," says Davis. "But if there's a critical situation anywhere on the battlefield, I'm going there." Sometimes the Marines set up a satellite headquarters closer to the action; known as a "jump" command post, it allows the commander and other officers to move back and forth more easily between the main headquarters and a hot spot.

SAFETY IN NUMBERS?

Robert Lutz believes that one of the biggest mistakes made by U.S. business managers is blindly trusting market research instead of using their own eyes and ears backed by judgment and common sense. "One of the functions I hate in automobile companies is called product planning, which is a ton of left-brain guys sifting through reams and reams of market data and then coming up with an elaborate numerical model of the market that takes on for them the semblance of reality," he says. "The products they come up with are bland, run absolutely counter to

common sense, and almost always turn out to be disasters." Lutz
notes that Ford's market research indicated that consumers
wouldn't care much about a left-side back door on its minivans,
so the company didn't offer one at first. Meanwhile, over at
Chrysler, Lutz was observing that people with other types of
vehicles seemed to use their left-side back doors all the time, so
he ordered one up for the Chrysler minivans. The feature
became the biggest single factor in Chrysler's trouncing of Ford
in the minivan market throughout the mid-1990s.

Filter and Disseminate Information

In general, intelligence has been having a good day so far. Despite
high clouds that have blinded some "national assets," the Marines
have kept up a flow of information on the enemy's progress via "sen-
sor strings" airdropped in front of the enemy path. These strings
hold tiny devices, arranged like Christmas tree lights, that can sense
vibration, magnetic fields, heat, and other signatures of enemy vehicles. Intelligence has also managed to rack up "soft kills" on (that is,
to jam) many of the enemy's radio and radar capabilities. In fact, as
the Coyotes will later point out, intelligence has done too good a job
of jamming. Instead of blocking enemy communications and radar
outright, it can be better to block them intermittently at crucial
moments, so that the enemy continues to rely on them only to have
them fail when they are needed most.

Even better, word soon buzzes through the command tent that an
intelligence team has intercepted an enemy radio message. The intercepted message (sent by a Coyote posing as the enemy) turns out to be
one reporting 50 percent casualties in an enemy unit hit by a Marine
artillery shell. The intelligence group doesn't pass the message on to
the battalions right away. Though commanders are always eager to
know how much damage their strikes are causing, so they can adjust
their fire accordingly, this particular message by itself wouldn't help
them because it doesn't make clear which artillery battery fired the

shot. Only when that piece of information is established do the intelligence officers relay the message to the relevant battalion.

This sort of information filtering is the rule for Marines. "Collecting information is only 10 percent of the intelligence battle," explains one Coyote. "How you disseminate it is 90 percent." To avoid getting bogged down with information, Davis has asked for "exception briefing"—that is, to be informed only when something important hasn't gone according to plan. In addition, he has specified "the commander's critical intelligence requirements"—the enemy data that, if unearthed, could prove crucial to the mission. One example is the location of enemy artillery batteries. Every Marine is trained to be aware of these top-priority intelligence requirements and to pass any information relating to them immediately on up the chain. An oft-heard mantra among Marines is: What do I know? Who needs to know it? Have I told them yet?

CORPORATE INFORMATION WARFARE

Most businesses wrestle with an information glut, and the problem is getting worse with the availability of massive quantities of online data. According to a 1999 study by the competitive intelligence firm Fuld & Company in Cambridge, Massachusetts, companies use as little as 30 percent of the online business data they purchase.

VeriFone has long been a big believer in the importance of information filtering. Will Pape, the company's chief technology officer for fifteen years and a former journalist, used to take it on himself to pore over the reams of data generated by the company's activities—as well as those of its customers, competitors, suppliers, and the various governments with which it dealt—each evening, then composed a succinct summary of the critical information that he e-mailed to every employee in the company. When the company went public in 1991, the practice was hampered by SEC insider-trading rules that tightly restrict the distribution of sales data, but VeriFone adapted by registering 348 of its employees as insiders—more than any corporation in the country, including companies 100 times its size.

Perhaps surprisingly, companies can sometimes legally engage in certain forms of jamming, in a broad sense. Consider HealthSouth Corporation, whose stock price was being pushed down in 1999 by a string of Internet stock-trading bulletin-board postings that were spreading false rumors. The company hired private detectives to track down electronically the people posting the messages, then sued some of them. It even engaged in a type of selective jamming in that it continued to monitor the messages of some of the posters without letting the posters know it had identified them.

Identify the Most Likely and the Most Dangerous

As part of the planning process, MAGTF officers have spent time trying to figure out which pieces of information would help them decide between courses of action during the battle. Knowing how much damage the enemy's advance guard has sustained, for example, helps commanders determine when it's time to pull back the light armored vehicles and tanks. The more planning time available, the more alternative courses of action can be analyzed and linked to needed information. But no matter how short the time, Marines set a minimum level of analysis: they want to have straight in their heads at all times the enemy's most likely course of action and its most dangerous course of action—that is, the one that would pose the largest threat to the Marines' success. Thus, the only time the Marines risk being relatively unprepared is when the enemy does something that's both unlikely and not especially damaging. By definition, this won't happen very often, and when it does it shouldn't present a serious problem. On the other hand, when the most likely and the most dangerous scenarios coincide, Marines know they have to pull out all the stops.

Employing good intelligence and planning techniques to anticipate various enemy actions allows the Marines to have potential responses thought out and ready to roll. The resulting rapid reaction times can be devastating to an opponent's efforts to follow its own plans. The Marines refer to this reaction time, and to the time between successive strikes against the enemy, as "operational tempo." "The idea behind using tempo," says Zilmer, "is to be causing things to be happening faster than the enemy can react to it. You want to be able to capture, collect, process, categorize, and act on more information about the enemy than he can about you. You're operating on a faster cycle than he is."

PRINCIPLE #24: MAKE TEMPO A WEAPON

Tempo is not the same as speed. A group might be able to carry out a task quickly but then require a delay before determining what its next high-speed task is, resulting in a slow tempo. By the same token, a group can maintain a brisk operational tempo even when carrying out each individual task in a relatively slow fashion. A Marine squad normally doesn't rush when carrying out a patrol, for example, lest the squad hurry right into a killing field, but sending patrols out one after another maintains a high tempo. Randy Gangle notes that the ability to keep up a rapid tempo directly depends on a willingness to push authority down to the front lines. "Under the old system, if a unit achieved a breakthrough and displaced the enemy from a location it was told to take, it had to wait for new orders," he says. "Now the unit can exploit the enemy's vulnerability and keep going after another target."

HEADING OFF COMPETITIVE THREATS

Amazon has employed tempo effectively by adding new product categories at a rate its competitors can't match. In a twelve-month period beginning in mid-1998 the company expanded its offerings at its bookselling site to include greeting cards, music, videos, toys, auctions, and electronics, and it also got into the online pet supply, prescription drug, and grocery businesses.

AT&T, meanwhile, offers an illustration of watching for a convergence of the competition's "most likely" and "most dangerous" actions. Consider how aggressively the company responded to the threat to its core business of phone-line–based communications services posed by cable companies, which can provide not only television programming but also high-speed phone and Internet services. When the cable giant MediaOne went into play in 1999, AT&T outmaneuvered a host of other major contenders to acquire the prize, ending up with what promises to be broadened leadership in the communications arena.

MISSED PLANS

This morning, as the hours pass, all the complexities of integrated maneuver warfare rise up and haunt Davis and his MAGTF. O'Neal privately ticks off for me a small catalog of mistakes and problems: because the MAGTF didn't bring along enough rocket-assisted artillery shells to reach all the enemy artillery batteries, the enemy will be shelling the Marine ground forces; it didn't make airstrike decisions quickly enough to provide the aviators with the thirty-minute lead time they need to prepare the jets; it used some of its most powerful bombs against the enemy's flimsy reconnaissance vehicles instead of saving them for the much larger and more heavily armored forces that followed; it stayed engaged with the enemy's advance guard in front of the canyon too long, taking losses that will leave the MAGTF weaker than hoped when it confronts the enemy's main guard inside the canyon—the main effort.

It's far from unusual for plans to go awry in this way, especially with the sort of complex, integrated maneuvers practiced at 29

Palms. O'Neal observes that Davis has committed a planning error typical of visiting commanders here: anxious to cover his bases in anticipation of different enemy responses, Davis and his team spent time developing four artillery- and air-support plans that spelled out in detail exactly where and when the fire was to be directed. The problem with detailed plans, says O'Neal, is that no matter how many you develop, none of them ends up precisely fitting the scenario that unfolds in the field. The enemy reaches a certain point sooner or later than anticipated, or suffers fewer casualties than expected, or has more artillery than was known about. These are the sorts of surprises that have occurred today, and because the plans were so detailed, recalculating the fire plans was too big a job to handle on the fly.

Rather than trying to come up with a number of plans that each apply to one situation, says O'Neal, it's better to have fewer plans—two would have been plenty today—and to keep them simple enough to be broadly applicable and quickly modifiable to a wide range of situations. The specifics can then be tailored to the situation that arises without having to throw out or rework the plans.

PRINCIPLE #25: KEEP PLANS SIMPLE AND FLEXIBLE

WHATEVER WORKS

As an example of the importance of planning flexibility in business, the MIT economist Paul Krugman argues that the U.S. economy has greatly outpaced Germany's in recent years because the same obsession with extensive, rigid planning that has made many of Germany's products—such as its automobiles—so desirable throughout the world has also left many of its businesses unable to adapt to rapid shifts in technology and markets. "Americans, by contrast . . . go with whatever works," he writes.

Realistically, the MAGTF now has little chance of accomplishing its original goal of demolishing the enemy when it's inside the canyon, says another Coyote, Captain Peter Lazarus. But that doesn't mean the MAGTF has to walk away with a failure. "The overall mission isn't doable with what they've got compared to what the enemy still has," he explains. "Now they've got to figure out which smaller pieces of the mission *are* doable. If they only have the ability to engage in one good fight, then they need to see where the terrain will support them and make the most of it." To that end, he adds, the MAGTF needs to manage carefully its dwindling supply of artillery fire and air missions and focus them on supporting that one battle. "I counted nine targets designated in one square click," he says. "You can't fire everywhere. You have to pick a killing area."

The MAGTF does in fact wisely focus on taking out the enemy's remaining air defenses, and it finally succeeds (with perhaps a modest amount of fudging from the Coyotes, who are the ones who determine when an enemy unit has been disabled). That allows the Marines to send in the choppers that will carry ground troops to positions around the canyon to inflict heavy damage on, though not wipe out, the enemy. Soon the word goes out on the radio net: the objective has been achieved. That seems a generous assessment, but after being tough on the MAGTF throughout the week, the Coyotes now seem interested in ending today's exercise on a note of mission accomplished.

DEBRIEFING

As sunset approaches, the Coyotes' Hummers arrive from different directions and land on a flat patch of desert the size of a football field. The group gathers around O'Neal to discuss how they should conduct the "hot-wash," or debriefing session, to be held with the MAGTF officers, who will be arriving in a few minutes. The Coyotes don't formally evaluate the MAGTF, but they want to make the day's events as useful a learning experience as possible. (The Coyotes also periodically provide suggestions to Marine headquarters for improving the teaching and practice of combined-arms combat tactics and send out a quarterly bulletin for all Marine battalions on weaknesses they've observed in visiting MAGTFs' efforts.)

O'Neal has each of the few dozen Coyotes responsible for one of the MAGTF's units give a thirty-second assessment of that unit's performance. Though by almost any armed force's standards the MAGTF did quite well, the Coyotes know what perfect planning and execution look like, and the list of the MAGTF's difficulties quickly grows long. Though each Coyote takes pains to find something positive to point out about the unit's performance, O'Neal starts to become concerned that the hot-wash is going to be dominated by a demoralizing "firehosing" of Coyote criticism. But one of the last Coyotes to speak reports that the light armored vehicle unit performed flawlessly. "A bone!" shouts O'Neal, elated. "Let's make sure you go early in the brief." Hummers and tanks start pulling up, so O'Neal brings the Coyote conference to an end.

During the hot-wash a Coyote major diplomatically asks LeSavage, Davis's executive officer, whether he feels that the MAGTF's actions against the enemy's main body were completely effective. LeSavage starts to discuss where the efforts went astray, but before he can get far Davis steps in and starts to explain that he himself made planning mistakes. This exchange represents a standard protocol: subordinates are given the opportunity to take the lead in the discussion and are given the credit (along with their Marines) for everything that went right, but blame for problems is quickly intercepted by senior officers.

Anything that happened during the day that didn't go according to plan—a category that covers much of the day's events—is red-flagged for further analysis that evening. It's going to be another long night. But when O'Neal ends the debriefing, the Coyotes express enthusiasm about the MAGTF's performance. It's not phony. The Coyotes know how many tries it took them to achieve their expertise at these difficult integrated maneuvers. And they know that almost every mistake made in the Palms 29 exercise today is one less mistake that will be made the next time these Marines get a shot at it.

Nevertheless, no matter how good the Marines get at any aspect of their mission, they never consider themselves to have reached a pinnacle. They always suspect that somehow there's a better way to do things. In the next chapter, we take a look at how the Corps nurtures a drive for change.

☆ ☆ ☆ ☆ ☆

10. ORGANIZATIONAL CHANGE

The status quo is going to lose.
—Colonel Robert E. Lee

A group of Marines, one of them a sergeant, is hiking up a long, steep hill under a vicious Camp Pendleton sun. The sergeant's mission in this simulated exercise is to have his squad take out a mortar pit that, he was told, is at the top of the hill and has been firing on a nearby helicopter landing zone. Two-thirds of the way up the hill the sergeant is informed that his squad is under machine-gun fire from the top of the hill; the mortar is in fact on the next hill over. After directing the squad to take cover, the sergeant mulls over his options. His first inclination is to have his squad continue up to take out the machine gun, having come this far, before heading over to the next hill to get to the mortar. But then he considers the commander's intent, which was to protect the landing zone on which the mortar was firing. This consideration suggests that the appropriate move is to go directly to the mortar, since the machine gun can't shoot far enough to threaten the landing zone. On the other hand, reflects the sergeant, his mission could also be jeopardized by leaving the machine gun in place, which could result in his squad taking casualties when they try to head back down.

As the sergeant thinks out loud, a man stands nearby listening and taking notes on a clipboard. Though he has been trying to keep in the background, he couldn't stand out more from the Marines with whom he has been tagging along. He is slight, bearded, bookish-looking, and dressed in shorts, white shirt, and running shoes. His name is Gary Klein, and he is a psychologist who has been hired by the Marines to design for them entirely new approaches to battlefield decision-making training.

If there is something incongruous about the idea of an academic helping to run a combat exercise, it is exactly the sort of incongruity that the Marine Corps seeks out. Because as effective as the Marines' principles and practices have proven, the Corps is constantly on guard against becoming stagnant or constrained by an inbred point of view. "Today's solutions are tomorrow's problems," says Captain McBreen.

How does an organization reconcile a heavy grounding in tradition and core philosophies with a drive to change? As usual, rather than being fazed by the tension between seemingly contradictory character-istics, the Corps finds a way to derive strength from it. In this case, the answer lies in creating an atmosphere in which change becomes a con-stant in its own right. "Making adjustments is part of our tradition," explains Brigadier General Lee. "Within the broad framework of estab-lished policy is the opportunity for individuals to institute change."

RETOOLING DOCTRINE

In the 1970s, notes Lee, many politicians and experts argued that the U.S. military should move away from the tradition of having a "doc-trine"—that is, a formal codification of organizational practices, such as a standard procedure for defending an island. The Soviet military, pointed out the experts, had all but strangled itself by adhering to a strict doctrine. But Henry Kissinger, echoing the feelings of the Marines on the subject, defended the idea of a properly applied doc-trine. "Kissinger said that doctrine can provide flexibility because it sets up boundaries within which you're freed up to take initiative," explains Lee. "Without doctrine, you have to spend time figuring out what game you're playing."

In other words, an appropriate doctrine can leave plenty of room for creativity while preventing the sort of confusion and gross inefficiency that would probably result from having no formal guidelines whatsoever as to how the organization operates. With the Marines, says Lee, doctrine not only makes room for initiative but also embeds within it a mandate for occasionally stepping outside the doctrine and ultimately changing it over time. "Having been on numerous awards boards, I can tell you we don't just tolerate pushing boundaries in the Marine Corps," he says. "We reward it."

PRINCIPLE #26: MAKE DOCTRINE A LIVING THING

It's not easy creating an organization of people who understand that though they are expected to take the rules seriously they are also expected to break them occasionally and eventually to tamper with them. "If you're not careful, you can become a hostage to your own doctrine," says Colonel Zilmer. "The only thing harder than changing doctrine is giving up the new doctrine once you've accepted the changes. We try to make that change part of the process by ingraining in our people that we prize ingenuity."

Needless to say, the Marines don't want to create an organization in which everyone feels free to break the rules whenever the spirit moves them. As Zilmer notes, the line between becoming a slave to established practices and losing the efficiency and discipline they provide can be a thin one. "You don't want to depart from doctrine until you understand it well and recognize the risks of departing from it," he says.

REVOLUTION BURNOUT

Professor Eric Abrahamson of Columbia Business School, who studies the ways in which business managers try to institute organizational change, offers a broad indictment of corporations' current fascination with entirely reinventing themselves on a semiregular basis. "Current prescriptions for change routinely recommend the most destabilizing, disruptive approaches, ignoring the place of each change in an ongoing series of changes," he says. "These approaches may be pulled off once, or at most a few times, but repeated attempts to undergo massive change result in burnout, cynicism, and chaos. Continuous revolution failed Chairman Mao in the People's Republic of China, and it will fail corporate America. The solution is to balance change with stability."

RELENTLESS RESEARCH

To make sure that they know what they're doing when they alter doctrine, the Marines have long made a practice of dedicating groups of people to exploring new approaches to combat and other missions as well as new management techniques. As this research pays off in workable concepts, the new approaches and techniques are incorporated into Marine practices on an ongoing basis. As a result, the Corps is essentially undergoing constant, gradual change. Though the change can ultimately be quite significant, it tends to happen one relatively small step at a time. In this way, the Corps has avoided the long cycles of stagnation punctuated by massive, painful, and often fruitless restructuring and big-bang reengineering into which many businesses have fallen. Says Kirk Nicholas: "The last thing we want to do is throw the organization into chaos and take a long time getting back up to speed."

This tradition of incremental change has produced some of the modern world's most significant innovations in warfighting. After World War I the Marines set out to find a way to make amphibious warfare workable. Up until then assaults on well-defended beaches had been considered suicidal, and after disasters such as Britain's costly 1915 battle at Gallipoli, other military forces remained uninterested in making such assaults part of their repertoire. By the time World War II broke out the Marines were ready, and though their phenomenal string of victories in the Pacific islands came at a high price, the Corps virtually on its own shifted the balance of power in coastal warfare from the defender to the attacker. The Allied forces borrowed these techniques in the D-Day invasion, setting the stage for victory in Europe. After World War II the Marines pioneered the "vertical assault"—attack via helicopter insertion—which has since become a mainstay of the U.S. Army and most other major military forces.

In recent years the Corps has actually stepped up its commitment to experimenting with new approaches to combat, organizational structure, and management. "We're not afraid of change," says Bedard. "Everything is a point of departure for us."

PRINCIPLE #27: EXPERIMENT OBSESSIVELY

In 1997 the Marines decided to create a more formal vehicle for innovation in the form of the Warfighting Laboratory, based at Quantico. To research new approaches to combat, the lab puts together experimental units—the "MAGTF-X"—that run exercises with new equipment and techniques. Randy Gangle and a group of MAGTF-X officers went on an unusual field trip: "We realized we need to get a better understanding of the special complexities of cities, so eighty of us walked around Chicago for a few days. We saw the critical nodes to be attacked and defended: the water works, power plants, communications facilities, tunnels, bridges. How do you go about securing a power plant? Then we just looked at the thousands and thousands of people walking around everywhere, and the lightbulb went on: if we do things in this environment the way we normally do, we'll be killing a lot of people who don't deserve to die." Other groups of Marines, he notes, went to other cities so that all the groups could compare notes.

Gangle points out that the lab goes out of its way to avoid stacking the MAGTF-X with elite Marines. "If we can't make things work

for the average Marine, then what's the point?" he says. For that reason, as well as because of a general belief in the ability of most
Marines to come up with good ideas, the Corps doesn't limit the
focus on invention to the lab. In fact, in spite of its emphasis on
instilling confidence and pride in its people, the Corps also encourages Marines to feel the need for change. As Major Perry puts it: "A
lot of our leadership programs are status quo, and nothing fails like
success. How can we do better?"

TECHNOLOGY

Like most organizations, the Marines have felt the impact of the PC
explosion. PCs have replaced stereo systems as the electronic appli-
ance of choice in the barracks, phone lines are tied up by Web surfers,
and in the slightly seedy commercial strip outside the Quantico
Marine base General's Java Internet Café seemed to be holding its
own against the more storied Hawg & Dawg across the street.
According to one colonel, some 90 percent of all Marines—including
virtually all officers—now have regular access to the Internet.

This computer boom has presented obvious opportunities for online
training and routine communications. In addition, newer versions of
larger weapons are increasingly computer-controlled or -assisted. A new
generation of Howitzers coming into the Marines, for example, are run
primarily by keyboard. Some new weapons are designed to be operated
almost exactly like video arcade games, complete with joystick and buttons. "These kids have grown up with the eye-hand coordination skills
for this sort of thing," says Lieutenant Colonel Allison. "It's second
nature to them."

TWITCH TRAINING

Bankers Trust found that its conventional training classes were
literally sleep-inducing to some of the bank's young hires—

many of whom could sit riveted in front of a Nintendo game for hours at a time. The solution: the bank developed training software that provided some of the same information as its classes, but in a video-game–like context.

The Marines are also embracing a wide range of combat and weapons simulations systems—not so much to replace traditional exercises as to supplement them. We looked at the squad leader's course simulation in Chapter 1. Another system allows different weapons to be fired, from the standard M-16 rifle up to an 84mm rocket launcher, at a large screen that displays full live-action video of enemy soldiers and vehicles in a number of different scenarios from open-ground maneuvers to embassy attacks and night-vision–assisted patrols. Needless to say, the weapons don't fire actual ammunition (though a grenade launcher does hurl a plastic grenade), but they are otherwise the real thing, rigged up with a pneumatic device that provides authentic-feeling recoil. For added realism, the weapons run out of "ammo" at the appropriate time and are made to jam occasionally. After the simulated attack, a computer tallies up the operator's "kills." The Marines are also experimenting with computerized mines that can discriminate between enemies and others and be remotely turned off when a conflict is over.

But the Marines aren't interested in merely making their existing weapons and practices more efficient. The Corps wants to take advantage of technology by designing new styles of warfighting around it.

PRINCIPLE #28: BUILD NEW TACTICS AROUND NEW TECHNOLOGY

Consider, for example, the Marines' interest in giving fire teams and squads the freedom to spread out and act autonomously, in line with the principles of maneuver warfare. The drawback to this autonomy is that individual units often can't quickly find out where other units are, and centralized command can't provide guidance based on the shifting progress of the overall battle.

To improve the situation, the Warfighting Lab is running a series of experiments with computer and communications technology that enables both central command and individual units to stay abreast of what's happening in the battle. One experiment had eighteen squads of Marines fanning out over 1,500 square miles of Camp Pendleton desert. The squads were equipped with hand-held computers, into which enemy positions could be entered, and global-positioning systems (GPSs) to track their own locations. The data from each squad were sent to a single command post—in combat it would be a ship—where officers could put together a coherent picture of the entire battle scene. In another experiment a MAGTF-X "invaded" San Francisco from the sea and received "support" from distant, ship-based Navy guns aimed by computers tracking both friendly and enemy positions. The goal of a new round of tests is to get enough information back to the squads so that they can make better decisions about where to call in fire. "It allows the squads to act like ground sensors for all the precision weapons we have coming on line," says former Colonel James Lasswell, a lab consultant.

The Marines are also working with MIT's Media Lab to come up with a hand-held computer that can understand human speech, both to save the time it takes to type a message and to allow officers to choose to hear the spoken versions of messages to judge the urgency in them. "For centuries soldiers have only been able to see what's going on in the battle by bringing their eyeballs to the scene," says Brigadier General Timothy Donovan, who heads the Warfighting Lab. "Now we're sending out recon teams with digital hand-held cameras that tag pictures with GPS locations. It will give us instant reporting that can take the place of putting Marines in harm's way."

Despite the enthusiasm for what new technology can do for them, the Marines haven't abandoned the spirit of doing more with less. According to Allison, Marines found out that the CIA had a number of small, flying drones for spying on enemy locations sitting in storage unused; the Marines picked them up for one-tenth the original cost and modified them for their own needs. More important, the

Corps has been aggressively trying to use off-the-shelf consumer technology rather than rely on custom-made devices. In addition to being vastly cheaper, consumer technology tends to improve far more quickly, going through new generations every eighteen months or so versus the standard five-to-ten-year military acquisition cycles. For one experiment a Warfighting Lab officer ran to a local Radio Shack and bought several walkie-talkies for less than $100 each; they worked better than the standard Marine models.

FASTER, CHEAPER, LESS CONTROLLED

It's not just military services and government agencies that can benefit from giving up a certain measure of control over the production of new technology in exchange for speed and cost savings. Even among leading computer manufacturers, whose product life cycles are ultra-short, there is growing recognition that the job of quickly and cheaply assembling, testing, and shipping products may be one best left to companies that specialize in it. IBM, Hewlett-Packard, and Mitsubishi are among the companies that have sometimes turned their backs on decades of tight management of production, looking instead to outside companies for the manufacturing of some products.

Marines are also maintaining their emphasis on people over equipment. They want to be able to use the latest technology without being so focused on it that they can't be effective without it. For one thing, high-tech equipment can easily become damaged or jammed by the enemy; even the much-vaunted F-117 stealth fighter proved unexpectedly vulnerable during the bombing campaign in Kosovo when Serbian antiaircraft batteries used relatively simple techniques to detect and shoot one down. The problems are even more serious with off-the-shelf devices, which, of course, aren't designed for combat environments. What's more, in times of fast action and high stress, frontline Marines often find computer and communications gear more distracting than useful and prefer to fall back on their eyes and ears; it's not uncommon for a squad leader who suddenly comes under fire to reflexively yank off his radio headset. In the mock invasion of San Francisco mentioned earlier, some Marines looked down at their hand-held computers only to read that their squads had been "killed" by mistracked Navy fire.

PRINCIPLE #29: DON'T DEPEND ON TECHNOLOGY

For these reasons, the Corps intends to keep training Marines in all the traditional, low-tech combat techniques, allowing the high-tech elements to serve as enhanced alternatives rather than out-and-out replacements. Marines being trained on the new digital Howitzers, for example, continue to practice plotting fire the old-fashioned way. "If you lose your technology, you'll always have a backup means for getting the job done," says Donovan. "You'll still know how to use a map and compass as well as a GPS."

Donovan also notes that being trained in both high- and low-tech ways of accomplishing tasks improves Marines' resourcefulness. He recounts the experience of a Marine infantry fire team that during an exercise found that its radio wasn't linking up to that of a nearby tank with which the team needed to coordinate. So one of the soldiers ran up to the back of the tank and wired up a phone connection. When the heat from the tank's 1,400-degree exhaust started to melt the wire, the tank crew figured out a way to deflect the exhaust. "These kids have tremendous motivation to accomplish the mission with whatever technology they have," says Donovan. In fact, he adds, the Marines only hope that their opponents make the mistake of becoming dependent on high-tech gear. "We'll be looking to exploit the enemy's information technology systems," he says. "We'll deny him services, put false information in, and even start telling his forces what to do."

Gangle, meanwhile, points out that most of the new combat techniques the Marines have developed in part to take advantage of new technology actually work well even without the technology. "I think we can improve effectiveness 70 percent without buying a single new piece of equipment," he says.

LEARNING FROM OUTSIDERS

The Marines recognize that one key to keeping up the pace of change and a flow of creative thinking is to get good input from outside experts and thus to avoid becoming insulated. By "outside" the Marines don't simply mean other military services, with whom they are constantly exchanging information. They mean a variety of institutions in the government, academic, and commercial sectors.

PRINCIPLE #30: GET AN OUTSIDE PERSPECTIVE

A simple example: the Marines have generally been treated well by Hollywood. One exception was *Full Metal Jacket*, the Stanley Kubrick film that portrayed Vietnam-era Marine life as psychopathic. The Corps' response? It asked Warner Bros. studio, which produced the film, to allow the Corps to use clips from the movie in a training CD-ROM it was putting together. (The studio refused, claiming concerns with piracy.)

The Corps' relationship with the psychologist Gary Klein is a particularly illuminating example of the Marine thirst for the sort of fresh, offbeat points of view from which the most influential new thinking often emerges. Klein had been doing research on decision-making in the hopes of coming up with a better way of teaching people to make decisions, and he had come to the conclusion that the conventional model of a rational chain of reasoning did not in fact reflect how decisions are usually made in most lines of work. "The rational model worked well in some cases, like when it came to deciding about whether a bank should approve a mortgage," he explains.

"But for most situations the model seemed wrong." To confirm his suspicions, Klein spent months interviewing firefighters and observing them in action. His conclusion: firefighters, and apparently most decision-makers, employ a sort of intuition to arrive at a course of action. Unfortunately, this intuition is developed solely out of personal experience, Klein determined, and can't be taught to others—leaving Klein with no obvious way to build on his discovery. "I was in a rut," he says.

Then one day Klein received a call from a Colonel Tony Wood from the Marines Warfighting Lab. Wood had read Klein's papers, he explained, and was convinced that Klein was right; moreover, Wood believed that Klein's intuitive decision-making model perfectly fit the Marine view of battle. Wood got right to the point: Would Klein put together a weeklong course within the next two months that would teach intuitive decision-making to Marines?

Klein found it hard not to laugh. He wasn't sure which aspect of the request was the goofiest. That such a course could be taught in one week? That it could be taught to twenty-three-year-old grunts? That it could be created from scratch in two months? Klein simply offered the most obvious objection: the whole point of his theory was that decision-making can't be taught at all. Wishing Wood luck, he declined.

"I'm sorry to hear you say that," said Wood. "I guess I'm going to have to get someone else to do it."

"I don't think you understand what I'm saying," said Klein. "It's not just that I won't do it. It's that it can't be done. It's impossible. *No one* could do it."

"All I'm asking, son," said Wood, "is that you give it your best try."

Having thus been exposed firsthand to the Marines' skills at recruiting and motivating, Klein found himself working on a course to teach what he had concluded was unteachable. When he was finished, he told Wood he would give the course a try, but he wanted to start with senior officers. "Never mind us colonels," said Wood. "It's the squad leaders that count." The result is that Klein now teaches decision-making to businesses, aviators, Army officers—and Marine squad leaders. "It's all because that colonel insisted it was doable," he says.

The goal of Klein's teaching process is to turn decision-making trainees into what he calls "reflective practitioners"—that is, people who can think about and articulate the elements that contribute to their decisions. He prescribes that one-third of all exercise time be spent in debriefing. At Camp Pendleton, Klein gives an example from a simulation exercise earlier in the day. "A squad is hit by artillery," he recalls. "The leader tells them to run for cover, and one of them steps on a mine, so two people are killed, and it's like ringing on the enemy's doorbell. Afterwards I asked the squad leader: Was he aware there was an artillery spotter? Was he aware of other assets? Was he aware of the risks? What information does he wish he had? Does he know how he'd do it if he were in that situation again?

"I love working with Marines," Klein adds. "A lot of Army people go through entire careers without doing anything in an operational setting, making it easy for them to come up with ideas based on how they think things ought to be. Marines have enough of an experience base to know traditional models don't apply. They're eager to improve, they're open to criticism from inside and out, and there's an expectation at all levels to wrestle with ideas. At most organizations there's a tendency to work hard for five years or so and then shrink back from risk. Here people are always looking for a challenge."

To get yet another perspective, the Warfighting Lab sent officers to Wall Street to hang out with financial traders. The goal: to learn how to make fast decisions based on information flowing in through banks of monitors—which may be exactly the way colonels operate in future conflicts. Though the experience was helpful—the traders taught the officers, for example, to make better use of split screens—Lasswell notes that there's a limit to how much the Marines want to emulate the traders, given a fundamental difference in the way they view end states. "The traders are happy as long as they win more than they lose," he says. "When losing means you bring home bodies, that's not good enough."

Perhaps the most surprising idea under consideration for obtaining an outside perspective is that of bringing civilian business managers into the Marines as instant colonels or at other high ranks. Though such managers wouldn't have the benefit of such unique experiences as OCS and The Basic School, the Marines are quick to admit that the outside world may have expertise and management solutions that can be translated to their own needs—and they don't necessarily want to wait to grow it on their own. Besides, notes Major General John Admire, the Marines and the business world have at least one thing in common. "Whether you're pursuing peace or profit," he says, "there's a lot of tough competition out there."

The Marines, at least, are ready for it.

SOURCES

All the information directly pertaining to the Marines in this book came from firsthand interviews and observations, with a few exceptions, such as the occasional tidbit gleaned from news reports.

The following articles provided information used in some of the business examples. Most of the rest of the information for these examples came from firsthand interviews, or else is credited in the text. If I've inadvertently failed to credit any source, I apologize.

Abelson, Reed, "Silicon Valley Aftershocks," *New York Times*, April 4, 1999

Anders, George, "Webvan Taps Bechtel Group for Facilities," *Wall Street Journal*, July 9, 1999

Ball, Jeffrey, "But How Does It Make You Feel?" *Wall Street Journal*, May 3, 1999

Bank, David, "As Microsoft Matures, Some of Its Top Talent Chooses to Go Off-Line," *Wall Street Journal*, June 16, 1999

Bradsher, Keith, "Behind the Labor Peace at Ford," *New York Times*, March 21, 1999

Carey, Susan, "Frozen Northwest," *Wall Street Journal*, April 28, 1999

Dao, James, "A Kingmaker Takes No Prisoners," *New York Times*, January 18, 1998

Deutsch, Claudia H., "A New Kind of Whistle-Blower," *New York Times*, May 7, 1999

Fisher, Lawrence M., "On-Line Grocer Is Setting Up Delivery System for $1 Billion," *New York Times*, July 9, 1999

Flynn, Laurie J., "E-Commerce Twist: Full-Service Shipping," *New York Times*, July 12, 1999

Gomes, Lee, "At Microsoft, a War Smolders Between Haves and Have-Nots," *Wall Street Journal*, August 10, 1998

Gomes, Lee, "Upstart Linux Draws a Microsoft Attack Team," *Wall Street Journal*, May 21, 1999

Hafner, Katie, "Coming of Age in Palo Alto," *New York Times*, June 10, 1999

Harmon, Amy, "With the Best Research and Intentions, a Game Maker Fails," *New York Times*, March 22, 1999

Hays, Constance L., "Advertising: Coca-Cola's Former Advertising Philosopher Sees the End of Marketing as He Knows It," *New York Times*, May 24, 1999

Helyar, John, "Solo Flight: A Jack Welch Disciple Finds the GE Mystique Only Takes You So Far," *Wall Street Journal*, August 10, 1998

Hymowitz, Carol, "Criticism Is a Cinch; Try Telling Employees How Good They Are," *Wall Street Journal*, July 6, 1999

Hymowitz, Carol, "How Amazon.com Staffs a Juggernaut," *Wall Street Journal*, May 4, 1999

Hymowitz, Carol and Murray, Matt, "Raises and Praise or Out the Door," *Wall Street Journal*, June 21, 1999

Karr, Albert R., "Work Week,", *Wall Street Journal*, May 18, 1999

Kravetz, Stacy, "Work Week," *Wall Street Journal*, July 6, 1999

Krugman, Paul, "Why Germany Kant Kompete," *Fortune*, July 19, 1999

Lancaster, Hal, "Today's Free Agents Work at Twitch Speed," *Wall Street Journal*, October 6, 1998

Leutwyler, Kristin, "Dilbert's Corollary," *Scientific American*, October, 1998

McCartney, Scott, "Upstart's Tactics Allow It to Fly in Friendly Skies of a Big Rival," *Wall Street Journal*, June 23, 1999

Miller, James P., "A Top Black Executive at McDonald's Steps Down to Join Buyout of Supplier," *Wall Street Journal*, May 9, 1999

Moss, Michael, "CEO Exposes, Sues Anonymous Online Critics," *Wall Street Journal*, July 7, 1999

Munk, Nina, and Oliver, Suzanne, "Think Fast!" *Forbes*, March 24, 1997

Murray, Matt, "Late to the Web, GE Now Views Internet as Key to New Growth," *Wall Street Journal*, June 22, 1999

Nelson, Emily, "Logistics Whiz Rises at Wal-Mart," *Wall Street Journal*, March 11, 1999

O'Neil, John, "He Thinks He Can, He Thinks He Can," *New York Times*, April 6, 1999

Orwall, Bruce, "As Web Riches Beckon, Disney Ranks Become a Poacher's Paradise," *Wall Street Journal*, June 9, 1999

Petzinger, Thomas Jr., "The End of Leadership Is One of the Myths of a Gloomy Time," *Wall Street Journal*, September 18, 1998

Petzinger, Thomas Jr., "Why They're Thankful: Glowing Research, a New Trading Model," *Wall Street Journal*, November 27, 1998

Pollock, Ellen Joan, "Falling Stars," *Wall Street Journal*, January 5, 1999

Quick, Rebecca, "Retail, Like War, Is Hell at The Limited," *Wall Street Journal*, April 21, 1999

Ramstad, Evan, "How Trilogy Software Trains Its Raw Recruits to Be Risk Takers," *Wall Street Journal*, September 21, 1998

Samuelson, Robert J., "We Aren't All Free Agents," *Newsweek*, June 14, 1999

Schultz, Ellen E., and Auerbach, Jon G., "IBM Pension-Plan Changes Spark Ire-Filled Web Site," *Wall Street Journal*, June 14, 1999

Sebastian, Pamela, "Business Bulletin," *Wall Street Journal*, July 1, 1999

Seglin, Jeffrey L., "Saving a Life but Crossing a Line," *New York Times*, November 15, 1998

Sellers, Patricia, "The Aya-Cola Speaks, and We Can't Help But Listen," *Fortune*, July 5, 1999

Shafer, Ronald G., "Jacket Flak," *Wall Street Journal*, February 19, 1999

Shapiro, Eben, "Time Warner Defines, Defends System of Values," *Wall Street Journal*, April 9, 1999

Thomas, Paulette, "A Tavern's Fame Spreads Hand to Hand," *Wall Street Journal*, March 2, 1999

Thurm, Scott, "Digital Now Beats Analog in the Sale of Cellular Phones," *Wall Street Journal*, December 4, 1998

Thurm, Scott, "Solectron Becomes a Force in 'Stealth Manufacturing,'" *Wall Street Journal*, August 18, 1998

Webber, Alan M., "Are You on Digital Time?" (interview with George Stalk Jr.), *Fast Company*, May, 1999

Wilke, John R., and Bank, David, "Microsoft to Face Tough Claims of Unfair Tactics Against Java," *Wall Street Journal*, December 1, 1998

Wysocki, Bernard Jr., "Trading Up," *Wall Street Journal*, December 1, 1998

Zuckerman, Laurence, "The Jet Wars of the Future," *New York Times*, July 9, 1999

THE MARINE CORPS MANAGEMENT PRINCIPLES

1. **Aim for the 70-percent solution.** It's better to decide quickly on an imperfect plan than to roll out a perfect plan when it's too late.

2. **Find the essence.** When it comes time to act, even the most complex situations and missions must be perceived in simple terms.

3. **Build a capability-based organizational mission.** Focusing on developing organizational talents creates opportunities; focusing on particular products and services invites obsolescence.

4. **Orient to speed and complexity.** The ability to react quickly and effectively in chaotic environments usually trumps other competencies.

5. **Organize according to the rule of three.** In times of stress, most people can efficiently handle exactly three key responsibilities.

6. **Build authority-on-demand into the hierarchy.** Retain a strong management pyramid, but encourage people even at the lowest levels to make whatever decisions are necessary to accomplish the mission when management guidance isn't at hand.

7. **Focus on the small team.** Most of the organization's critical tasks are accomplished by the lowest-level managers and their subordinates, so anything done to make them more effective will have a large payoff.

8. **Task-organize.** The size and make-up of groups within the organization should be changed according to the needs of each specific mission.

9. **Hire via trial by fire.** Challenging a prospective employee makes it easier to determine the fit, and initiates a bond between the hiree and the organization.

10. Employ extreme training. Situations faced on the job shouldn't seem more daunting than those faced in training.

11. Breed decision by analogy. Managers can't be briefed on every possible situation, but they can be trained to recognize similarities between novel and familiar situations.

12. Cross-train. Running through different jobs creates versatile managers who understand all aspects of the organization, even if at a cost in efficiency.

13. Manage by end state and intent. Tell people what needs to be accomplished and why, and leave the details to them.

14. Distribute competence. Obsessively and ceaselessly educate and train people at all levels of the organization.

15. Reward failure. Someone who never fails probably isn't pushing the envelope.

16. Make personnel functions stepping-stones for stars. The development of the most promising managers should include taking responsibility for hiring, training, promoting and transferring people.

17. Glorify the lower levels of the organization. The higher the manager, the harder he or she should work at making it clear that the rank and file are the heroes.

18. Demand to be questioned. Subordinates should feel free to openly disagree with their managers, up until it comes time to carry out a final and legitimate decision.

19. Instill values that support the mission. The ability to get the job done can be a function of shared character.

20. Cultivate opposing traits. Success often requires combining seemingly contradictory approaches.

21. Establish a core identity. Everyone in the organization should feel they're performing an aspect of the same job.

22. Match strength to weakness. Find ways to tilt the playing field to the competition's disadvantage.

23. Surprise and disorient the opposition. A confused and off-balance competitor can be routed with fewer resources.

24.   **Make tempo a weapon.** Controlling the pace of competition can exhaust and demoralize the competition.

25.   **Keep plans simple and flexible.** It's better to have a few options that can be easily adapted to changing situations than to try to make specific plans for every contingency.

26.   **Make organizational doctrine a living thing.** It's good to standardize practices, as long as one of them is to continually refine and occasionally change the practices.

27.   **Experiment obsessively.** Even the most successful organization will eventually stop winning if it doesn't explore radically new approaches.

28.   **Build new tactics around new technology.** Fully leveraging technology requires new styles of competing.

29.   **Don't depend on technology.** Train to be effective regardless of which technologies are available.

30.   **Get an outside perspective.** Insights into organizational improvement can often come from people in seemingly unrelated fields.

INDEX